The Best Little Girl in the World

A memoir of endurance

C. C. Clark

Dedication

I would like to dedicate this book to my grandmother, who stood by me with honest words and encouragement when I felt all hope was lost. No matter what I did, I would always be accepted and loved by her, even when I thought she wouldn't approve of my actions or decisions. She has inspired me to be: "The Best Little Girl in the World."

Acknowledgements

I would like to thank Celia for a decade of friendship, Michelle for truthful words, Tamieka and my mother for listening to all my frustrations and guiding me through this book. My mother's thoughtful words provided a different perspective that I needed to see. I wouldn't have been able to write this book without their help. They helped me when I thought life was too much, and they watched me grow from this experience. I would also like to thank my grandmother for giving me the tough love and encouragement I needed to write this book, and my dear friend Grim for her editorial skills and great times in PDX. I would also like to thank Professor Sue, who explained skills that couldn't be seen with myopia.

Introduction

'Ché, sit still, so I can do your hair"

"Mom?"

"What Ché?"

"Why can't I be white? Why can't I be pretty with blonde hair and blue eyes? It always hurts so much when you comb my hair. I bet if I was one of those girls on the TV my hair would be a lot easier to comb."

Across the room, a commercial was playing on our TV: the women were holding surfboards and beers, with their hair blowing in the wind so fine and smooth. This was the first time that I had voiced that I wanted to be white and it wouldn't be the last time. My mother started to rip through my hair while screaming at me to never say such things. When I tried to reach up and hold my scalp, she popped my hand with the comb, and then hit my face.

"You should be proud that you are black. What the fuck is wrong with you? I think you need to go to your grandmother's house. Wait until she hears this shit!"

The only thought I had at that time was that being black was a burden. I didn't want to be black anymore. I wanted to be white, to have friends, and *not* to get beaten up anymore. I didn't want the Hispanic kids picking on me anymore by telling me it was okay because they weren't as dark as me and spitting on me every day on the bus after school like I was dirt. *What was so wrong about wanting to have friends? What was so wrong about wanting to be white?* I understood very quickly as a child what it was like to be an outcast and not having even one friend because I was black.

During my first years of school, I was bullied, beat up, and spit on like I was nothing. The other kids asked me daily whether I had washed myself the night before because "We can't tell because your skin is so dark." Instead of spending my first years making new friends, I learned what the meaning of *racism*.

When I heard that a mulatto girl named Tiffany was coming to my school, I was so happy. I thought I would finally have a friend, but I wasn't prepared for how deep *hatred* goes, and no child can be.

When recess came on Tiffany's first day of school, I ran outside to meet her. I just knew we were going to be best friends. I saw my newfound friend standing alone in the middle of the playground. I ran up to her and introduced myself. Her skin was so light that she could almost pass as a little white girl if she didn't have dark freckles and tight thick ringlet curls around her face. She looked at me in fear, almost as if she had found out before I could befriend her that I had the *black disease*. Before I could even whisper a hello, I saw Jen and Jessica running across the playground towards us.

"Get away from her. If you play with her, we won't ever be your friends!" Jen screamed across the playground. Before they reached us, I asked, "You won't be my friend,

Tiffany?" I already knew so much about my new friend from eavesdropping on other children.

She looked at me, pitying me, and in a voice not above a whisper said, "I'm sorry. I can't."

Jen then exclaimed, "If you stay close to her any longer, she's going to turn you dark, too! Then no one will want to be your friend either!"

I watched her run away from me like I was the *plague.*

"I don't get it, she's like me so how come she can be your friend and I can't?"

Jessica spouted, "Duh, she's not as dark as you, stupid. When she gets out of the bathtub she knows when she's clean and you don't. She's only half-black so she's only half as bad, whereas you're full black and everybody hates you."

The tears were already falling down my chunky cheeks, and so I ran to the building and sat against the wall waiting to get called in from recess, hugging myself and pretending that I liked myself. When you're a child, you see things in a different light. You don't think of things as being *racist.* You think of it as you're the one who is ugly, that you don't belong, and that you will never belong.

Chapter One

Only one other time in my life did I say that I wanted to be white—after I was incarcerated.

"Ché, is there anything else that I can help you with?" Sandra, the county jail guard, asked me.

"Can you make me white? Can you make me blonde with blue eyes, because this wouldn't be happening to me if I was!"

Sandra just looked at me in horror, like my secret was out.

I went into my 8x10 cell and cried to God. I cried that he should have made me white, that he made a mistake. I was supposed to be white, so did he forget? Did he forget about me in the midst of all the people he created? I wasn't supposed to be this ugly dark thing despised by classmates. I was supposed to be the best little girl in the world—at least that's what my grandmother would always say.

What had happened to me, the best little girl in the world? Dreaming of my grandmother, I could almost pick up the scent of White Diamonds (her favorite perfume) drifting across my face as she bent down to me and pinched my cheek asking, "Now, who is the best little girl in the world?" I would always respond with, "I'm the best little girl in the world."

Yet as I lay on the metal bed with an inch-thick mattress and held my knees to my chest with my back against the painted concrete walls, I no longer felt like the best little girl in the world. I didn't feel like the little chocolate drop or Lady Godiva that my family seemed to love so much. I felt like some indistinguishable black monstrous beast that no one wanted to touch, because I was too disgusting. I tried to comfort myself with thoughts of going to a prom. My mom wasn't able to attend her prom because of me, and so I wanted her to live vicariously through me. I will be out of jail before prom, then I will go to prom and be named prom queen and this will all go away. I kept telling myself, *this isn't real. I'm going to wake up from this and be at home getting ready for school in the morning.*

How did this happen to me? I am only 17, and I love playing volleyball. I don't even have my driver's license yet. What college I wanted to go to? The previous quarter, I had finally made honors. My mind started racing over the past two or three years of my life. *How did I get here?* I kept trying to search my mind for an answer. The only thing that came to mind was the last argument I had with my mom about living with my father.

Chapter Two

My mom, two younger brothers, and I had just moved back to Columbus, Ohio, where I had been born at St. Anne's hospital in Franklin County. This city is where the majority of my family on both sides resided. I thought living in the same city with my dad and that I would be able to see him more. He had already spent 10 years of my 13 years in prison.

I had lived with him during my sixth-grade year. When he registered me for school in Wisconsin, they didn't require any paperwork, but when we moved to the Columbus, they wanted my birth certificate, social security card, and immunization records. He didn't have any of these documents, and so I couldn't get enrolled in school in Columbus. I spent half a year out of school because my mom refused to give him the documents. She thought it was crazy for me to still be living with him almost a year after she sent me to him. I had to move back to her, but ended up living with my grandmother.

I loved my grandmother and her peach house by the railroad tracks. Every night, I could hear the trains come by and the house would shake a little. I had returned to the place where I didn't have a single friend. It was different this time when I lived with her. She would wake me up every morning to get ready for school while she got ready for work. I would sit and listen to her old school songs until it was time for my bus. I enjoyed those mornings with my grandma, eating breakfast and helping her find her car keys, or lying in the bed with her and reading. It seemed she always felt what I was feeling, and I always felt safe when I was around her.

Then my grandparents started arguing and the new teasing started at school because I was the one of the two girls in my class to have early breasts. My utopia was coming to a quick end. I developed an eating disorder to ignore the fights in the house, which involved more screaming. I finally figured out that they were arguing about me. I decided to move back with my mom instead of living with my grandparents because I didn't want my grandma upset all the time. I didn't want the constant bickering about how to raise me. I asked to move back with my dad, but it wasn't an option.

When I was with my dad, I didn't feel like a piece of junk mail that got dumped in the garbage. I felt like I was part of a family, like a child. I had been living from house to house like a lost piece of mail being returned whenever the recipient felt like I was no longer needed (usually my mother). My relationship with my mother was just crumbling into a fiery pit the older I became. All I wanted to do was protect myself and my brothers from her, but I wanted to escape her grasp more than anything. I didn't want her choking the life out of my childhood any more. I had gotten a taste of childhood while I stayed with my father and I didn't want to go back to being my mother's personal maid. I wanted to go outside like the rest of the kids and play sport or be in a choir—anything but sitting around the house all day.

Unfortunately, by this time, my father had decided to move back to Wisconsin with his newborn son, Darren. He wanted to take me with him, but my mom (I thought at the time) was keeping me from him. Eventually, my mother moved her boyfriend down to live with us and this is when she felt it was appropriate to finally let me go stay with my father. Hindsight now tells me that this was the biggest mistake in my 13 years, but what did I know then? I knew that my dad loved me, and that I could have a seemingly normal childhood. I wanted to be able to go outside and play with the other children, and not stay cooped up in the house all day wondering when the next time my brothers and I were going eat something.

I moved back to the little town of Fennimore (population of 2,809), where I was the only black child in school again, and probably the only one for at least a 30-mile radius around town. The next few years of my life were as normal as I could get from a teenager's life, just going to school, playing recreational sports, and working until I turned 15.

Darren's mother, Teri, hated me since the birth of her child. She hated when I spent time alone with my father, but I didn't have him for the first 11 years of my life. When I first met Teri, we were best friends. She would let me curl her hair and we'd watch movies together, but it all changed so quickly when my brother came along. Teri's hatred for me grew to the point that I would just come home from school and shut myself in my room. Everything I did was wrong, and she would always let me know by complaining about me to her friends on the phone.

The real argument came when my dad wanted to give me his 1991 Chevy. I couldn't understand why she was so against me having that car. I worked, played a sport, and sometimes didn't get home until 11 at night because of the games or work. I wouldn't have to walk alone at night or sometimes get rides from them. One night after a game, I stayed outside and waited for them until midnight because I didn't even have a key to get into our home. If I had a car, I could've gone to a friend's house and waited until they came home.

I even told them I would pay for the car, but since the car was in her name we needed her permission. This argument about the car issue must have been her last straw. She argued the point that she wouldn't even get her son a vehicle when he turned 16. We all knew that was a lie. The constant fighting over the car was too much, and I gave up, but it had finally gotten to the point where she just flat out told my father that I wasn't her responsibility and it was either her or me.

My dad had, as usual, stayed out all night and left me with his girlfriend. He came in around 7 a.m. the next morning and I heard them arguing. He had to choose: either I left or she would take his son and leave. I didn't understand what I could possibly be doing that was so horrible that I had to leave. I wasn't disrespectful to her or calling her names. They screamed for almost half an hour, then I heard him stomping up the stairs. I jumped out of my bed and ran to my bedroom door to catch him leaving through front door.

"You can leave, too. Fuck this shit! I'm sick of this shit, I'm sick of you two always complaining about each other. You need to call your grandmother and have her come get you. I'm not doing this stupid shit anymore. Who the fuck do ya'll think ya'll dealing with?"

This would be the only warning sign that my grandmother would get. I walked the mile to school, tears blurring my vision. Still not comprehending everything that had happened, how could he not want me anymore? I wasn't a bad kid? I was a good girl. I walked into the empty school hall because, as usual, I was late. I took the left down the long corridor to the counselor's office. I asked him if I could call my grandmother to come get me and that I couldn't stay with my dad anymore.

"Sure, Ché. What's going on at home? Is there a problem?"

All I could tell this man, this stranger, was that my dad told me that I had to leave and I needed to call my grandmother to come and get me. I couldn't tell him the truth as it would soon be all over town. It was such a small town that everybody knew everybody and what everybody was up to.

My day was just a blur after that. I walked home regretting having to walk through the door. I couldn't help but wonder if I was going to walking into another battle. I was still thinking about the quick conversation I had with my grandma who said, "It's not a problem. We will come get you right away. Just call me when you get home, so I can get directions and talk with your father."

Luckily, no one was home when I got home, which was usual. Normally, I spent the majority of the time by myself. Teri had friends and family that she visited often and my dad was just around town. I grabbed the cordless phone and went to my room, which was on the first floor next to the living room. We lived in a triplex and our unit was on the end. At first glance, it resembled a ranch home, but all the units had the same layout. There was an upstairs and downstairs. In the basement, there were two bedrooms on the right side and a half-bath on the left, with a back door to the backyard. My room was above their room.

I kept calling and calling my grandmother, but no one was picking up. *Does she not want me either?* I just sat on my bed tormenting myself with thoughts of how I wasn't wanted at school or by my family. *What would happen to me?* My concentration broke when I heard a bass in the distance, getting closer to the house. I opened my bedroom door to catch my dad jumping the stoop to get in the house.

"Ché! Ché! Did you call your grandmother, yet?"

The tears started to burn my eyes, hot and turning red. My cheeks started to flush as he strode across the dining area and in three steps was by me. All I could do was nod that I had called her.

"Ché, I'm so sorry. I didn't mean what I told you earlier. I was tripping baby, but you see this bitch is going crazy, don't you? I don't want to lose you or Darren, but what am I supposed to do?" he started pacing the floor. "Fuck that, fuck her. She ain't shit. Let her leave, then we'll be straight. Ché, if she leaves, I'm going to need you to step up for me, okay? Do you understand that?"

The tears had dried on my gleaming face. My daddy did love me. He wasn't just going to kick me out because this woman hated me for no apparent reason. She taught me the importance of being the only child. Once, she had his child, the honeymoon was over, and there wasn't a reason for her to be nice to me any longer. I wasn't needed again. I looked at my dad and told him proudly, "Well I can help! I can help pay bills, too! I'm working now, so I can ask for more hours.

"Yeah…Yeah" he kept pacing in deep thought. That's the last memory I have of that school year before summer break.

The summer started and I got my driving permit. My dad thought it would be a good idea to go back home to Ohio where all of our family was and take a break from Teri. Then they could figure out what they were going to do because I wasn't leaving as she had hoped. I was secretly hoping that we wouldn't go back to Wisconsin. I prayed that he could get himself together back home by getting a job and enrolling me in school there. It might have worked if he had gotten a job, but all I could remember was him having a job with a construction company for a few months and that was it. We left in the late afternoon when no one was home. I got dropped off at the bus station an hour and a half away from town, while he drove his motorcycle to Ohio. It never occurred to me where we were going to reside once we got there.

When I arrived in Ohio, he met me at the bus station with a short and stubby woman named Jodi with red hair that barely passed her shoulders. We went back to her house and this is where we stayed for the summer. Even with all the family I had there, I spent the summer in either a crack house with him or stuck in Jodi's house alone. I hated going to the "spot" where he dealt drugs. It reminded me of when I was 11 and he took to the same apartment complex using it as a scare tactic (it worked; sitting on the second floor stairs of an apartment complex, I watched a woman walk inside the building where he was sitting. She wore a tattered gray sweat shirt and cut-off shorts. He ran up the stairs and grabbed me and told me come down. He thought it was hilarious how this woman would do anything he said. She didn't have any teeth. I didn't think it was amusing, and I pitied her and her loss of self-respect. She didn't care what she had to do just as long as she got the drugs. She had just sold her babies' diapers to get her last fix. I sat there watching her and realizing the damage that drugs can do.) It was almost as if I wasn't allowed to see my own family.

My dad felt guilty about having me cooped up in the house by myself for the past couple of weeks and he decided to take a day off to show me where he used to live and visit family friends. We rode on his motorcycle through what seemed like the whole city.

Once we reached his old neighborhood, his house was in the middle of the cul-de-sac, all big, bright, and yellow. He started pointing out which of his friends used to live in which house, and when he reached Robert's house (his best friend) Robert's mother Annette came to the screen door. Annette resembled an older me, and I thought that was funny. My dad followed her husband James downstairs. I stayed upstairs and admired Annette's house, as we talked about my grades in school and my hopes of going to college. I knew that I wanted to major in biology. She told me that I needed to pick my GPA up if I was hoping for any scholarships. I just nodded, knowing that I needed to work a little harder in school.

After we left Annette's house, we made a surprise stop in front of a strip club on Main Street. I just stood by the bike in my little jean shorts watching all the women in their fancy dresses going in and out. I wondered if I would ever be attractive, as I had always been a chubby child and it seemed like the baby fat would never leave. He finally came back after 15 minutes and was ready to go. When we hit the main drag, all the lanes were clear, and I felt the bike accelerating then it popped up, like we were doing a wheelie—we *were* doing a wheelie—down Main Street. I clutched him so tightly that I almost pulled us both off. I was used to riding with him since I had ridden with him before but never while he popped a wheelie.

When the bike popped back down to the street, I heard him screaming at me not to hold him like so tight. The approaching traffic light ahead of us was green. I felt him tilt the bike to make a right turn and—all of a sudden—I was sitting up on the side of the street. When I looked up, the bike was almost in the middle of the intersection and he was about 30 feet to my right. I hadn't quite grasped what had happened yet as blood was trickling down my knee from a small gash.

My dad got up and grabbed the bike. His face was contorted in anger. An older man was sitting in his truck at the light and asked us if we were okay and said that we took the corner a little too fast. I was still confused about what was going on when father's voice started echoing in my head.

"This is your fault with your fat ass! Why the fuck didn't you lean when we were turning?"

I couldn't believe what he was saying to me.

"Hurry yo fat ass up, and don't fucking touch me either. You better hold on with those fat ass legs of yours."

During the ride back to Jodi's house, all I could hear was how stupid and fat I was and I better not dare touch him to hold on. I was so scared that I was going to fall off the bike. My legs had started going numb from trying to grip the side of the bike and hold on through the accelerations, and I started to slide off the bike. I kept hoping I would just fall off and die, but I wasn't that lucky that night.

When we pulled up to the brick townhomes, a pain hit my stomach. Not the kind when you're full or constipated, but a different kind of pain. It was my intuition that was telling me something bad was going to happen. I got off the bike and he was still cursing me. I held my head down and followed him up the concrete path, as he was fumbling to get the key out of his pocket. Seeing him upset wasn't bothering me as I had seen him upset before but he had never directed his anger at me. My mind started screaming at me for me to run somewhere, anywhere. Run to someone's house I knew my around the city or that I could call someone, my grandfather's house was just down the street, and it would probably only take me 15 minutes to get there. It was also after midnight and I wondered if anyone would be up, but before I could finish the thought the realization came that it was too late. As my hand reached for the screen door and started to slowly pull it back, I felt a burning sting come across my face.

I stood there wide eyed, not comprehending that my father had just struck me for the first time in my life.

"What! You didn't think I would hit your stupid ass! Get upstairs!"

Following orders, I just slowly trudged up the stairs, but I should have listened when my mind told me to run. He began to kick me all the way up the stairs. I didn't realize it was possible for a person to literally get their ass kicked all the way upstairs. I couldn't believe he was hitting me; first we crashed the bike and now this. I couldn't do anything but cradle myself and cry. I went to the room that had a love seat and a mattress on the floor. I grabbed my pajamas and put them on to go sleep. He had disappeared into the other room, still screaming at me. I just wanted to go sleep so this would be all over. Turning the light out in the room, I laid down trembling, still flabbergasted by the evening's events. Then the room light flashed on, I glanced up to see him standing over me with a 9mm gun.

Before we left Wisconsin that summer, he had taught me how to shoot and handle a gun, so I knew when I looked at the 9mm I was in real danger, as the safety was off.

"Get up" he demanded.

I didn't want to move; I felt like I was paralyzed. I sat up as his hand came down with the gun and smacked me back to the ground. My mind started to wonder if I was going to die as he cocked the gun, making sure to show me that there were bullets in the chambers. He then pushed the barrel onto my forehead. I couldn't believe what was going on; I couldn't process everything that was happening. I couldn't even make out the words he was roaring at me anymore. Something about Teri wanting him to be home and not wanting to take care of me. I just sat there shaking. I sat there thinking if he didn't want to take care of me, why didn't he just send me away like everyone else? I got smacked with the gun a second time.

When I got up this time, I couldn't control anything in my body. I could see that he was punching me in my legs but I couldn't feel anything else. I didn't even feel myself pee. Then I heard the door close from downstairs as Jodi crept up the stairs. I thought it was over. He wouldn't do this with someone else around. Then I felt the cold metal go in between my legs. My pajamas were now soaked in urine and tears.

"Oh, you think she gone save you? She's going to do whatever the fuck I tell her to do and so are you!" he yelled.

I just tried to muffle my cries. Then he left and I heard them whispering. I just lay down to sleep like this was a nightmare that I would wake up from any second. He came back in the room and dragged me by my hair to her room. I was standing there looking at her naked on the bed.

"Lick her," he said in a sinister manner. *What?* My eyes must have asked the question for me.

Then my chest almost caved in from his punch. He pushed my face in between her legs and I did as I was told. I just wanted the night to end. I didn't understand what was happening. *Why was she letting me do this? Why didn't she call the police?* It seemed like hours had passed while I was down there, tasting her bitterness. I could no longer feel my legs. I could just hear her moans and feel her legs squeezing me.

Once he fell asleep and I tried to stand to go back to my room, but my legs wouldn't hold me. I pulled myself across the hardwood floor to the other room. I was still waiting to wake up from the nightmare. I lay back on the mattress that I had already urinated on and didn't care. I didn't want to wake anyone up. I just wanted to go to sleep like this day had never happened. I kept waiting for him to come and snatch me up like he had before, but I was able to cry myself to sleep. The next morning, everything was back to normal like nothing had happened the night before.

I still couldn't walk, as both legs were completely purple. He came in the room as if nothing had happened the night before—we hadn't crashed the motorcycle and he hadn't put a gun to my head. I sat there in amazement when he asked me why I couldn't get up. I started pulling my pajama tee shirt over my legs to cover the bruises and carefully told him the events of the night before. He thought I was lying, saying he couldn't remember anything after we had left Annette's house. I sat there and pulled my pajama tee up so that he could see the damage from the night before. All he could tell me was he was sorry and he couldn't remember anything, and he was really stressed out. After that night, I couldn't wait to go back to Wisconsin. I spent the rest of my summer locking myself in that room until we returned to Fennimore.

Chapter Three

It wasn't too long after we came back and I started school that the arguing began. This time it wasn't about me, but about money she had overspent. They had money to buy a game console and games for my three-year-old brother, but didn't have money for me to get new glasses. They just continued arguing until Teri had had enough of his abuse. This would be the turning point of their relationship. When Teri screamed out calling my father an "Uncle Tom" through the screen door, I saw my farther explode into this demon that I had only seen once before. He had just picked me up from school, and we were driving through the curved bend that framed the high school in a boomerang shape, and we pulled through it leaving the high school. A gray four-door Chrysler was coming in and out of the lane and when we got side by side, all I could hear was, "Fucking niggers!" The car whipped into a u-turn so fast that I was smashed against the door. I could hear the shifting of gears.

"Dad…Dad! What are you doing? Stop please just stop!" I pleaded. Luckily, the car had already twisted down the bend. My father was not satisfied, and we started lurking through the one-mile-long town trying to find this car.

"Ché, I understand you were scared, but you got to put all the crybaby bullshit to the side. You need to grow up. Don't ever let anyone call you out your name, spit on you, or put their feet on you. Do you hear me?"

"I don't want you to go back jail" I squeaked

"Well, I guess it was a good thing that one of us was thinking about the consequences" he murmured.

I heard the screen door almost being ripped from the hinges and that's when my thoughts finally snapped back as I heard the front door bursting open. All you could hear was them screaming together—Teri out of fear and him out of anger. I just sat in my dad's friend's truck until my dad came out listening to her screaming, just happy that this time it wasn't about me.

Teri moved after that night after letting everyone know that he had poured lighter fluid on her and taunted her with a lit Zippo. She came from a very prominent family in the town, so when she left everything just fell apart. We were kicked out of the nice pale-yellow triplex, and we weren't given a reason why had to leave. Ms. Mary Anne, as everyone else called her, would come to aid my dad again by letting us rent one of the green apartments at the edge of town.

Mary Anne was the one who assisted dad with getting a job at the town's biggest battery factory when he first lived in Fennimore. When he was released from prison for beating a police officer, they just dropped him off in the middle of Fennimore with no money and no resources to fend for himself. Mary Anne picked him up and gave him a home to let him get himself together.

At this time, my dad didn't have a job. We didn't have much money, so we worked off the deposit by cleaning out the other apartments. He was selling drugs to pay rent and keep up his own habits. School started to become more of a battle every day, I had to endure the smearing of my dad. Every time he was in the newspaper for traffic tickets, I had to hear about it at school. Then my classmates started arguing with me about how he was ruining someone's life by using drugs with them. As much as I hated going to school, I knew that I needed to go so that I would be able to go to college and get out of this god forsaken town. I got my job back at Hardee's and my dad would just take my checks for bills. I didn't really care about him taking the money, I was contributing to the household so that we could survive. Eventually my little Hardee's checks would no longer cut it and I would be presented with another job, from my dad as his mule.

"Ché!" I was sitting on the floor in the corner of the living room. I was just about ready to leave for school. Jodi was sitting across the room watching me.

"Yes, Dad?"

"I need you to do something for me."

"What?"

"Look, I need you to take the bus down to Columbus. You are going to pick something up for me, okay? Then you're going to come back, okay? I will be waiting for you at the bus stop when you come back, okay? When you get the package from Leon, just get right back on the bus. I don't care if you have enough money to go see your aunt or cousins. You stay at the bus station until it's time for you to leave. Do you understand?"

"What about school? What about my job? I have to work tonight."

I was confused. In reality, I was scared, and I didn't want to go. I knew what the package was and I didn't want any part of it.

"Why can't Jodi go. She's not doing nothing."

"What do you think that school is going to do for you? Is that paying the rent, Ché? Is it? I'm sick of this crybaby shit." He squatted down to eye level, and I didn't even get the chance to see his arm cocked. Just felt my face rippling in pain, after I hit the floor.

"Get up, get up, god damn it! You're going and I'm not listening to any more shit about it, you hear me?"

I couldn't hear him. The pressure from being smacked in the face made me temporarily deaf in my left ear.

"Are you fucking crying? Oh, hell naw! Bitch, I'm a give you something to cry about!"

I just balled up, as I knew more punches were coming. I felt like a punching bag for a professional boxer.

Jodi just sat across the room watching me and never saying a word. She was in another world. The punches finally stopped. I started thinking to myself that it was over. That's when I felt his hand grip my hair and pull me up to him.

"We are leaving right now, got it?

He gave me just enough money for the package and the ticket to come home. Half a day later, I was in Columbus, Ohio. Hungry and tired, I was given a description of a van when I called my dad. I sat outside and waited for this van to pull up. I remembered the prostitutes that I saw at the Chicago bus station, wondering if that was going to be me in a few years. My poor little life had taken a drastic turn for the worst since Teri was no longer with dad. I couldn't understand why Jodi couldn't take this trip. Why did I have to get involved? She wasn't working or doing anything useful in the house. I never really understood what Jodi's purpose was in our house. She was just there, just to simply be around Dad. As soon as we had moved into the green apartments, she moved in with us. I had no idea when she came that she had left her hometown to come to this town so that she could be with him or so she thought. Why do I have to be the one that's hungry and can't take a shower? I guess I could have just washed myself with the prostitutes back in Chicago, but watching too many "Pimps Up, Hoes Down" documentaries made me feel like I would have to fight for a sink.

Waiting outside for the van to pull up, I almost smoked a full cigarette. Walking up to the van, I started to worry about whether this was the right person or not. What if it was some creepy guy that liked little girls?

"You, B's daughter?" (Everyone knew my dad as B).

Once I had reached the van, I just opened the door and jumped in.

"Yeah" I responded.

"You are pretty bold to just jump into someone's van like you just did."

I guess he was right, but I didn't want to think of what would happen if I went back home empty-handed. We drove around the block for the exchange, and he dropped me off where he had picked me up in front of the station. I went back inside, bought a ticket to go home, and waited for the next bus to Chicago.

Chapter Four

When I got back, it seemed like our little apartment with the one couch and TV and VCR was becoming a night club. There was no possible way that I could sleep with the ruckus. Things seemed to have changed overnight. Everyone used to come over to smoke and drink, but dad had moved from weed to cocaine. This environment was a 360 from the one I was used to with Teri. I would spend many nights in bed pretending to be sleep so that I wouldn't have to interact with my dad's company.

One night, I got called out of the bed and walked into a crowd of normal people.

"Ché, I need you to move the stuff okay."

My dad said as he handed me the plastic bag full of cocaine. He had taken it out of its normal spot, which was in the room with me in the closet hidden in one of the jacket's inside pockets. I put it in the second bedroom across from my room in the light fixture. No one ever goes in this room. It was just an empty room. Not this night, though, and Jodi got sent to the second bedroom and after she turned the light on she never noticed that she was burning up all the cocaine.

Lying back down, I thought it would be nice if everyone left so I could get some sleep. I started to doze off when dad came in the room.

"Ché, what did you do with it?"

It had only seemed like it was a few minutes. When I went to grab it out of the fixture, it was gone.

He snatched my arm, "Where is it, Ché?"

I couldn't even stammer a response.

"God damn it, why don't you pay attention." He turned away from me and headed down the hall into the living room. I just stood there looking at Jodi as she tried to pick the cocaine crumbs off the floor. After he told the last few people that he was done for the night, everyone had to go. He came back to the room with this demonic look in his eye, pacing the floor.

"Do you know what you just burnt up?"

He grabbed my shirt so hard he scratched my chest through my pajama shirt. Then the chest shots came, and if there was one thing that I did learn from him, was to never cower and fall to the ground. I just stood there, my head felt like it was going to go flying across the room from some of the blows. Jodi just sat there, time after time, watching it happen. I couldn't help but wonder if she was getting pleasure from this. All of sudden it just stopped. I opened my eyes to see the wall.

I heard him using the bathroom, and so this was my only chance. I wouldn't get another one. I made a break for it, running out of the apartment through the backyard. By the time he figured out I had left, I was a couple of blocks away. I still heard his shrill screeching of my name. I had no idea what time it was, and I had no idea where I was going to go.

As I came out through one of the town's backstreet, I saw the apartments that the Bailey's lived in. Well, I guess I could see if Alisa, one of my classmates, would let me stay.

Unfortunately, Alisa wasn't home, but her sister Candace and her mom were. Her mom asked me if everything was okay.

"Of course, everything is okay...my Dad's just a little upset right now. Can I stay here tonight?" I asked them.

"Well, I don't have a problem with it. But tomorrow you will have to leave when everyone else leaves, got it?" Ms. Bailey said.

"Yes, ma'am." *What am I going to do?* The thoughts of him killing me just kept circling my mind. I could almost feel the cool 9mm against my forehead. I prayed that night that I wouldn't die by hand of my father.

Candace Alisa's youngest sister stayed home from school that day, so I didn't have to leave right away.

"My mom said you do have to be gone by the time she gets off work, which is at four." She said. "Are you going to tell me what's going on? Your face is pretty red. You know my mom was abused by her boyfriend too; it's okay, you can tell me."

Well, if you already know what is going on what's the point in me telling you? I thought.

"Nothing is going on, everything is fine."

"Well, I know it's not, but if you don't want to tell me, then I can't make you. Anyway, Alisa isn't really living here anymore. She's been staying with another family because she's not getting along with our mom."

I sat there thinking about my own mother and the two brothers I had left behind.

"Yeah, I don't really get along with my mom, either. Do you remember when I was here in the sixth grade? Well, my mom kicked me out."

"Are you serious?" Candace's eyes widen from disbelief.

"Yeah, I've been to see her once since I've been here, and every time I go back to her house even before I was staying with my dad, it just seemed like she was doing so much better without me."

"Why don't you just go stay with your mom?"

"That would be like jumping out of the frying pan into the fire. She doesn't want me at all."

I got up from the couch and started towards the door. I knew I was going to have to deal with the consequences at some point. Candace saw it all over my face.

"Ché?"

"Yeah?" I turned my sullen face back towards her in the living room.

"Isn't there someone that will take you?"

I mustered up a smile of courage and stated, "No, not anymore."

Walking home, I was hoping that by some miracle I wouldn't have to pay for my mistake. My stomach sank as I walked through the back door. I was staring at the paisley carpet as if it was going to turn into a magic carpet and whisk me away from this place. I knocked on the door and my dad came to the door.

"Where the fuck have you been?" he kept chuckling to himself.

I refused to tell him. No need to endanger anyone else's life.

"Well it doesn't matter anyway because I need you to go to Columbus."

My stomach started to cramp.

"You fucked this up so I don't want to hear shit about school or nothing. If I wanted to put yo ass on the corner to earn back the money you just lost, you better take that shit as a woman."

For some reason, this trip was different from the past couple. Something just wasn't settling right with me. Something just felt wrong. My stomach hadn't stopped cramping since I got to Columbus. When I met Leon this time, he asked me if I had eaten anything. I told him no. He saw me staring at a Sidney Sheldon book. He chuckled to himself as he bought it for me.

"You know your dad should be taking better care of you. You are still a minor."

This trip with Leon was different as well. We usually just met at the bus station and he gave me the package and I left. This time, I was able to admire his nice van, the kind of van that made you want to own it even if you didn't have kids. When I got in, we pulled off. I wasn't as scared of Leon as I had been before. He didn't seem like the type of man that would hurt me. Even though I had lived in Columbus a couple of times by now, I still didn't recognize any of the streets from the side of town we were on. We turned down a street right off of a busy main street, called Cadbury and it made me think of the bunny.

We pulled up into the driveway of a two-story brick house with a two car garage. Inside the house was even more beautiful. I just kept thinking to myself that I wanted a house like this one day. I had never seen a house so exquisite with a fireplace and vaulted ceilings. Everything looked like it had just come out of a home magazine into this house.

Leon turned to me. "Ché, why don't you go upstairs to the first room on your right."

I was still in awe over this beautiful house. I went upstairs to the first room on the right. It was a child's room, but I couldn't tell if it was for a boy or girl. There wasn't a bed in the room, just a bunch of toys that would be a good fit for a toddler. I started reading my book to occupy myself.

I loved to read, I would always imagine that I was a part of the book, just a character in the background watching all of the events, Leon called me back downstairs.

"Leon, you have a really nice house. I hope I can have a house like this one day."

He smiled and said, "You will if you work hard, Ché. You see my wife there is pregnant with twins. She's also a lawyer...a very good one at that. You can do whatever you want in this life. You just have to work for it."

The ride back to the station was quiet. I was still unsettled. I had learned to just suck it up, be quiet, and do as I was told. When I got out of the van, Leon looked at me, "Did you have school today?"

"Yeah." It almost seemed like he had this look of pity on his face.

"Ché, tell your dad to call me. He needs to take better care of you. Tell him I said that."

Halfway through the bus ride, Jodi called me, interrupting my decision on whether to pass the message along to my dad. If it was about me and I didn't pass the message, I would get beat, and if I did I would get beat as well, but I would have a better chance if the message came from Leon. I had a pre-paid phone for these special trips to let him know when I was coming back so I wouldn't have to wait so long waiting for someone to pick me up. The phone started vibrating but I didn't notice the first couple of calls. When Jodi finally got a hold of me, she said we were in trouble. She wouldn't explain anything else or where my dad was. She kept talking in this secret code that only she knew. She wouldn't say anything more, except my Dad wasn't coming to get me.

Just great. I took a deep sigh as if when I exhaled, all these problems would fade away. I thought, *I'm almost two hours from the bus station, how am I supposed to get home?* I called one of my dad's friends who went to school with me, Lil Phil. He was so cute with his baby-blue eyes. He was so slender, too, hence the nickname Lil Phil. He said he'd come get me. I had some comfort knowing that Phillip was coming to get me. I searched for reasons of why my dad wouldn't be able to pick me up. Once I arrived at the Madison greyhound station, I saw Brian's maroon Cougar glistening in the parking lot. Phillip came out to meet me. I asked him why Brian was with him. He explained that when I called, Brian was with him and realizing what I was coming back with volunteered to come.

When we got in the car, Lil Phil told me the events of yesterday. First, the house was raided a couple of hours after I left. Everyone was in jail, including my dad, but not Jodi. We were just coming out of the city when Brian noticed we were being followed. Phillip and I both thought that he was just paranoid, but after we started watching for a couple of miles, we knew he wasn't. Brian sped up to put a little distance between the vehicles. He made a sharp left turn on to a dirt road off of the highway. I gave the drugs to Phillip to throw out the window.

Brian was furious. "What are you two doing!"

"We can come back for it later!" Phillip screamed.

Brian kept speeding down this unknown county road. A black Blazer pulled out of nowhere in front of us, shot past us, and barricaded us on the road. A gray-haired stout man jumped out of the Blazer pointing his gun directly at the car.

"Hands in the Air!"

What was going on. We all had made a small pact to not say a word. The drugs weren't in the car and no one couldn't pinpoint where they were.

They separated us immediately. I got pulled towards the Blazer while Phillip and Brian were split between the two police vehicles parked behind the Cougar. An officer passed me a cell phone and my dad was on the other end.

"Ché, just give them the drugs."

I wanted to cry and did. I didn't understand what was going on. We were all taken to Dane County Jail. I gave them my statement of what little information I knew. Lil Phil and Brian were released that night. The officer asked me if I knew how much cocaine I was carrying.

"No."

"Well, let me tell you, Sweetie. You had 64 grams of pure cocaine on you. Do you enjoy being your daddy's mule?"

After I gave them my statement, I was taken to a half-way house that night for juveniles.

The counselors there couldn't believe what the officers were telling them.

"Why aren't you taking her to juvenile detention? She doesn't belong here if that's what she did."

The officers explained they had to put me somewhere for the night, and that everything would be cleared up tomorrow. The next morning, none of the staff understood why I was there. The counselors couldn't understand why I just needed a signature to be released. I didn't understand what was going on either. They all felt I should have been locked away, and then Jodi walked through the door and signed me out. On the hour and a half ride back, she explained that my dad was going to be released in a couple of days. They hadn't found anything in the house because she had just burnt everything up, and there were new drug dealers in town. Bubba, Lil Dwayne, and James had set my dad up. I guess this was payback for them trying to jump him, and him breaking Bubba's nose. I didn't like any of them. They just gave me a creepy feeling

Once Dad was released, the whole story was revealed. Justin, one of B's friends/customers, was put on a no-contact order from us and had to be escorted by the police to pick up his items out of the house. Dad made a deal that he would take the misdemeanor charges and serve his time. He would have to complete a three-year sentence. He also told on Leon, and now I was scared. It was one thing for my dad to want to live his life paranoid, but another for me. The truth started to come out about Leon. Leon wasn't really

Leon—he was on federal probation while dealing drugs and the FBI had been waiting to catch him.

I can remember that last conversation that B had with Leon, but he must have been telling Dad that he wasn't taking care of me properly because halfway through the conversation he started pacing and staring at me like I was a red cape and he was the bull ready to charge. The only things holding him back were the officers who recording the conversation.

"Ché, would you like to tell me what you and Leon discussed while you were down there?"

I just shook my head like I didn't know what he was talking about.

"Alright guys, I don't know what to tell you, I have to go down there instead of her if you want this done. I don't know what she did, but he doesn't want her to come anymore."

The officers all agreed that it wasn't a problem. If only they hadn't left me there. As we listened to the last car pull out the dirt parking lot and drive away from town, it wasn't a full minute before he launched his attack.

"What the fuck did you do, Ché? Can you explain to me why this grown-ass man is asking me if I'm taking care of my daughter?"

I didn't have an answer; I usually didn't at this point because any response was futile. There I was in the corner again, with him crouched in my face.

"Ché, why doesn't he want you to come down there anymore? What did you tell that man, huh?"

The back of my head felt like it was going to go through the wall, so whispering meekly, I said, "I don't know, I didn't tell him anything. He just bought me a book."

"Why the fuck is a grown-ass man you don't know buying you SHIT? Make me understand. Are you fucking that old man? You sucking his dick? What would make him say the shit he just said to me like I'm not taking care of you?"

I wanted to scream *you're not, you're not taking care of me*. I wanted to scream it so loudly that the whole town heard me, but it wouldn't matter because they already knew. I wouldn't dare defy him right now, as my head was already hurting. I could feel my right thigh going numb from the blows.

"I don't have time for this shit." That's all I remember him storming off and saying as he left me to cradle myself.

Chapter Five

It wasn't long after that summer that he had to turn himself in for six months. After it was published in the newspaper that our apartment had been raided, I, not surprisingly, was fired from Hardee's. The start of school was only a couple of weeks away and volleyball practice had started. Walking home from the first practice, I was completely exhausted. As I turned up the little hill to walk up the driveway, there was a blue Buick out front. Before I could reach the front door of the apartment at the top of the hill, Cederic came out of the apartment building door and my dad was following him. This didn't look good, not that Cederic was a bad boy, just that I knew he liked me. I was in the same grade with his sister, and the year before we had worked together at Hardee's before he stopped attending school. The look on his face made me even more uncomfortable as he was just gleaming with joy. Again, not that I didn't want him to be happy. I just didn't want it to involve me and, by the looks of things, it involved me.

He got in his sedan and said that he would be right back. As soon as the dirt was flying in the air from him skidding out of the parking lot, I turned to my dad.

"Ché, that boy really likes you."

I just looked at him. I felt like I had just been sold off like some prize cow. I had been one, and he just sold me off! I wanted to know what I was worth to him. How much did he get for me.

"I think you will be just fine with him,"

"What do you mean, Dad?"

"Ché, I'm going to jail in a couple weeks and I need to know that you are going to be taken care of. I know that goofy dude will take care of you."

At what price? I wondered to myself. I heard the bass coming from a car stereo in the distance.

"Ché, just go out with him for a little while. It will be just fine. He has a car."

As Cederic pulled into the driveway, I felt disgusted. He was a nice boy, just really immature, and a crowd follower.

I just stood there.

"Why don't you kids go for a walk?"

Cederic looked like he had just won a million dollars, a look of pure joy and excitement. I turned and started walking down the hill into town. I felt my tee shirt sticking to my skin because of the sweat. I started walking down the street, and I heard Cederic sliding down the driveway. In a couple of strides, he had already caught up with me. I still didn't have anything to say at this point. I was just hurt and speechless. *Who did my dad think I was?* You can't play with people's emotions. *What is wrong with him?* No matter how much he beats me, I can't turn into him, doesn't he understand that?

'Ché?"

"Yeah?" My face was parallel with the street as I wondered what was going to become of me. I had taken all of the required classes I needed for my junior year, so that, if I did have to come to school my senior year, it would only be for a class or two. Then I could work a lot more and figure out what school I wanted to go to. I didn't want to go to school there. I wanted to leave that God-forsaken town and never look back.

"I know you don't like me, but I think I will be able to turn that around. Even if you never do end up liking me, I'm okay with that because at least I got to spend this time with you."

My head shot up, and I turned and looked him dead in his face. He had this calming look in his eyes that maybe, just maybe, things were going to be okay. I would make it out of that town in one piece. I felt a warming flow through my body, the kind you feel when you step out of a shadow and into the sun, almost as if it was warming your soul. It tingled throughout my body. In that moment, I felt safe with him. I would never have this feeling with anyone else.

The following weeks leading up to my dad's incarceration were full of emotions. Watching him return to jail was the most heart-breaking situation for me. He had already spent the first 10 years of my life in prison and watching him go back and forth to jail was almost too much to bear. It made me feel like a toddler years ago that couldn't understand why daddy had chains on his hands and feet. Why couldn't he leave this place and come home with us. Then they dragged him out of the building into the car screaming like a banshee. It felt like I wasn't important enough for him to get a job.

Dale didn't think so. Dad had trained Dale to box professionally off and on for the past year. I remembered their conversation like it was yesterday.

"Man, B, I got to give it to you. You love your family so much that you risk your freedom to take care of them."

"No, Dale you got it twisted. You love your family so much that you are willing to work and listen to people treat you like shit all day so that you can provide for your family."

I didn't understand why my father couldn't just get a job like everyone else. He got into these long explanations about how unfair the justice system is, how he couldn't find a job. I always thought it was because he wasn't trying hard enough and that he wanted to sell drugs as a job, and that he wanted to be paranoid all the time. He didn't want to be normal like I wanted to be normal. As a child, if you have a parent who is constantly using drugs recreationally, the line between recreational and addiction becomes blurred.

A couple of days before my dad turned himself in to complete his first sentence, it seemed like Cederic had moved in with us because he was always there. One day, Cederic wasn't there all day to my surprise and I didn't think anything of it. That evening, Cederic showed up with Devin. I remembered Devin being in my history class the year before for a day and never saw him after that. He kept eyeing me like he had a secret to tell me, like we shared an intimate joke that only the two of us knew. He sure didn't waste any time getting on my dad's bad side.

"Ah, man, what ya'll got over there?"

"What? Ah, dude, just mind your business. You came in with Cederic and I suggest you stay where your friend is at."

The house was full as usual.

"What ya'll got over there? Ya'll smoking up some coke? Let me get some."

For once, my dad's bulging eyes weren't on me. I knew that stance though, and if Devin had any sense he would leave.

"Eh, Cederic, get your company and leave."

"Who the fuck is the mutha fucker coming in my house asking too many fucking questions"

"Is you working for the police, dude?"

"Naw, I'm not working for the police."

"Get the fuck out my house, dude" Oh shit, his right leg was behind the left and he would have been across the room in a single leap.

"Cederic, I think you should go. Just drop your friend off and come back later, okay." I said it so quickly, but Cederic heard the urgency in my voice. I, of all people, knew when my dad starts tugging on his sweatpants, he is about to attack like a cobra sizing up its prey. Devin kept locking his gaze on me. I felt like a mouse cornered by a snake that was toying with its prey.

This wouldn't be the last time I saw Devin. Cederic wasn't moving,

"I'll leave when Josh moves away from you."

Rumors were going through the town about my relationship with Josh being more than friends with me, which was true, so I understood why Cederic felt so intimidated. Josh lived on the corner from our old place with Teri. We were in the same grade. I met him through Teri's nieces that I used to hang out with and we also worked together at Hardee's. I loved spending time with him.

"Fine! Just go."

I turned to Josh, "Can you move down the couch so they can leave?"

Finally, they started for the door. After Devin went out first, Dad called Cederic back into the apartment.

"Eh, dude, don't ever bring that mutha fucker back to my crib, you understand me?" "Yeah. I understand. I didn't mean for any of that to happen."

This was the only response he could muster up. His eyes were still locked on Josh. Cederic knew we had a history together, and he hated it. It was almost like it tormented him. The next day, we dropped my dad off in Lancaster at the jail. The 10-minute ride back to Fennimore was done in complete silence.

When we pulled up to the green apartments that I stayed in, Cederic tried to comfort me.

"Your dad won't be gone long. It is only a couple of months."

"That's not what I'm worried about. I have to get another job, soon."

I was thinking about the fact that I was left with no money for me to eat or pay any bills. This bitch Jodi wouldn't take care of me. She showed me that last summer when we were staying with her in Columbus. I will never forget that night. That night will always be deemed the motorcycle night and will be the reason why I will never get on another motorcycle in my life. It was the taste of pain that was yet to come. I didn't have time to be thinking about this now.

"Why don't we try to get hired at Cabela's? If we get put on the same shift we can all chip in for gas, and you need a job anyway. You don't go to school right now or anything. What are you going to do with yourself? Are you going to go to college?"

"Well, I haven't really thought about it." What about colleges? Have you thought about that?"

"I was thinking that I would just go to South West Technical College and pick up a trade." He had the most innocent look on his face where you would have thought you might have been talking to a child.

"I'm not going to school here."

"Where are you going to go?"

"I don't know but it is going to be far away from here. Some where I belong"

"You don't think you belong here?"

"I know I don't belong here or I wouldn't be scared to go to school. You don't know what it's like to be the only black thing moving in that school." This brought back a conversation I had previously had with Heidi Loom, the school's star athlete.

"Ché, you act like you are scared to walk home by yourself."

" I am."

"Really? Why?"

I didn't have an answer for her. I just shrugged and ran toward the ride I was getting home, but walking home alone in the dark was not my favorite activity or being left outside my house waiting for someone to come home. I would have nightmares of being beat like the little girl in "To Kill a Mockingbird" happening to me, except no one would find my body.

Before school started, I quit the volleyball team. No one seemed to care that I had lost my enthusiasm. I just wanted to move on, past this town, past the last couple of years of my life. Once school started, I just didn't want to go anymore. I only had a couple of classes that I even wanted to go to: Ms. June and Mr. Hass classes. I hated chemistry, even though I enjoyed the subject. Mr. Will had a way of teaching that just made sense to me. When we were in class one day he explained ions. As he was passing back our quizzes, Lisa looked over at my score.

"How did you get that score?"

"What do you mean?" My voice dropped really low. Lisa was the kind of friend that you loved to hate. She was always in the middle of drama, always.

"Well, oh, you didn't do better than me so I don't care."

"What the fuck is that supposed to mean? Are you trying to say I'm stupid?"

Mr. Will tried to interject before it got hostile but it was too late.

"No, it's just that you never come to school is all."

"So I have to be stupid?"

"I mean if you would come to class, then you wouldn't have to take other people's notebooks"

"Are you talking about me taking Nancy's notebook?" Nancy was in my math class with Mr. Hass and when I didn't come to school, she would usually let me borrow her notes so that I could catch up, except this particular time she wouldn't let me. After she forgot the math notebook in class, I just took it home thinking I would just return it to her after the weekend.

"Yeah, she had to write that whole report over again because you supposedly found it in the park, which she never went to."

"Okay, so what I took her notebook so I could write my math notes. If Nancy has a problem, she needs to speak up for herself instead of sending her guard dog"

I started glaring at Nancy waiting for her to say anything. She had turned completely red. The whole class was watching us.

"I just don't get it, Ché. I had a project due and all of a sudden three days later you find my notebook in the park. It rained all weekend, so why wasn't it wet?"

"I took it. Nancy. I took your notebook for your math notes, shit, I'm sorry."

"I don't think so. I think you wanted me to do my project all over again."

"Why would I gave a fuck about your project?"

"Why did you take my notebook?"

Mr. Will stepped in, pulling me outside.

"Ché, you need to calm down. You can't be in my classroom cursing like a sailor, okay? Just let it go."

Stepping back into the class, I realized it wasn't over for me as Miss Lisa was on a roll.

"I just don't get why you can't come to school? You live in town so you can walk."

I could feel my body heating up like it was on fire, my fists were clenched so tight I could feel my nails imprinting in my palm.

"Why are you bothering me, Lisa?"

"I just think you're a liar, and that you lie about everything."

"Really?"

"Yeah, just like you telling Ms. Ray that I was cheating off of you and that's why you wanted to move away from me."

"I was lying about that, huh? You weren't cheating off of me on the tests?"

"Well, anyway I heard you've been spending a lot time with Cederic this summer. What's going on with the two of you?"

It seemed like it was planned. The timing was too perfect because as soon as it passed her lips, Joe, a senior in Cederic's class ran into the classroom.

"Look what I got here, it's a love letter for you, Ché, from Cederic," grinning like a Cheshire cat. I heard voices coming from down the hall.

"How can he even like her she's so dark, but that's probably the best he'll ever get." Not a second later, Cederic jumped in the classroom and snatched the letter from Joe. Mr. Will's expression said it all.

"What's going on here? You guys get out of here. You seniors, don't you have a class to be in?"

"Oh, my God, look at her face" a voice from the back said. All eyes turned on me. My face had turned flushed re, from the embarrassment of this love letter and anger that was just filling my chest.

"Wow, Ché, your face did turn red. Are you embarrassed? I didn't think your face could change colors."

That was my final straw and she got the response she had been waiting for. I jumped out of my chair.

"What are you fucking try to say, you blonde bitch!" I said it with all the anger at the top of my lungs. I wanted her to say it. I wanted her to say anything to give me reason to jump on her and show her why I don't come to class. I don't come because my bruises are visible. I don't come because I have grown-up shit to do. It almost felt they could see the steam coming out of my face. The whole class jumped up, "OOOOHH!"

"Oh, you are lucky the bell just rang."

I wasn't even talking to Lisa at this point. I had lost who was saying what and now I was in an argument with Grace. *That's it,* I thought to myself, *I'm not coming back to school here.* I will just retrieve my assignments from my teachers and that's it. Ms. June had already expressed how she didn't understand how I could miss so much school and still do so well on the assignments. Mr. Hass wasn't as forgiving. Had he not been so attractive, I probably wouldn't have made it to class as much. I finally found a job after school had been going for a month or two.

Once I started working at the hunting store, we started to get caught up on the bills. Jodi didn't think that I, being a child, should tell her what to do with her checks since she was the adult. She would only pay the rent and any left over money she spent on herself. We were all going to work for the first couple of weeks, until Cederic just didn't want to go anymore. I'm not sure if it was he didn't want to go anymore or if something else had his attention. He lost his job first, then Jodi just quit because she didn't want to work two jobs. She also didn't want to pay any of the bills either. I think Devin had something to do with Cederic not wanting to work anymore.

Devin started picking me up from school in Cederic's car after Cederic started taking courses at a near community college to earn his high school diploma. Cederic tried explaining to me why he wasn't attending our high school anymore, but I didn't understand what he was trying to tell me. Devin slowly started coming to the house on a regular basis, despite my father's warning.

Devin took me out to his grandmother's apartment in Lancaster one day after we dropped Cederic off at school. He asked her if he could have her check and she said that she was fine with it. When we left, he asked me to cash the check since he didn't have a banking account. How naïve I could be at times, because I sincerely believed everything he said. I didn't know that his grandmother didn't have the money in her account. I didn't know she was senile with Alzheimer's either. I had to pay the bank that money, which left Devin owing me the $500 that was taken out of my account. This was the start of the rollercoaster ride with Devin.

Chapter Six

Things just weren't going right: there was no food, we couldn't get caught up on bills, and I started getting drunk every night. How this was accomplished since I was still 16 at the time, I'm not sure. Devin started popping over my house whenever he couldn't find Cederic. He came over one night and asked if I would give him ride to the town bowling alley since Cederic was asleep. He had a friend that was going to give him some money. I waited patiently in the car for him to come back and a couple minutes later he strolled back to the car and said his friend wasn't home. Of course, I didn't think anything of it. Then the next day, I found out that he had broken into the bowling alley and stole whatever he could.

We didn't see him again until he had spent all the money. Devin came over explaining how sorry he was he didn't pay me back the money and bought me a bracelet. Supposedly, the diamonds were real and worth way more than he owed me. The next day, his mother showed up at my door asking if I had it. She knew that he had been hanging out around my house so she figured she would ask. I told her that he gave it to me for payment for the $500 that he owed me. I gave it back to her after she explained that he stole it from her. In a couple of days, I saw him again, when he popped up right before Cederic was supposed to leave for school. We just dropped Cederic off at school and drove to the new department store in Lancaster.

As we were walking into the store, Devin asked me if I knew that Cederic wanted to marry me. I didn't know. I didn't understand why we were even talking about this until I heard "Don't marry him, Ché."

"Why?"

"Because we should get married; even if you do get married to him, you know I'm going to be the one that pays for the ring, so it'll be like you are marrying the both of us anyway."

"I guess." *Where is this coming from?*, I thought. Cederic's secret was out now, so I confronted him in front of Devin.

"I wanted to do it the right way with a ring and everything"

"You don't even know me well enough to get married to me."

That evening Devin asked for a ride to Muscoda, which was a small town 10 minutes away. We all went so Devin could pick something up from another friend. We parked right off of the main street behind an abandoned building.

Once Devin left, we started fooling around in the backseat, and when we saw lights we just laid down since neither of us were decent. When the lights left, Cederic looked up and exclaimed it was the police. I hurried to put my clothes on as Devin came back to the car a few minutes later. As we started to leave town, the car was surrounded by the police. Devin started coaching us to say he didn't get out of the car.

We all went to the police station. This was the warning that I should have heeded. Once I was alone with the officer, he asked when he pulled up to the car why he didn't see us. I explained we were laying down, and I couldn't answer anything else because I didn't know anything else.

He looked me dead in my face. "Ché, I'm going to explain this to you. You need to tell me what happened here, okay? Because I'm going to tell you what's going to happen. Devin is going to keep committing crimes, but you will take the fall. Do you want that? If not, then you need to tell me what you guys were doing out here so late."

I wouldn't say a word. We were all released. Devin kept asking us what we said. I just went to sleep on the ride home not giving him an answer.

The next morning, Devin was pounding at the door. I opened it and he demanded to know where Cederic was. I told him he wasn't here.

"Well, your boyfriend told on me. So let him know I'm going to get him back." He turned from the door and was gone.

I called Cederic as soon as he left.

"Did you tell on him?"

"No, I didn't I don't know what he is talking about."

"He seemed pretty convinced that you did."

"I didn't." I stopped talking to Cederic for a couple days, trying to figure out everything that was going on. How was I getting involved in Devin's madness?

Later that day, I received a call from Diane, one of my dad's exes.

"Ché, I just wanted to tell you that Cederic was hitting on me."

"When?"

"Last night."

"I'm at Heather's if you want to come talk to me about it."

"Okay, I will be over there in a few minutes. I walked the mile to the other end of the town to the trailer homes. It was quite ironic that Cederic's parents lived right across the street from them. I walked up to Heather's trailer. The long walk didn't even cool me down a bit. Diane came to the door and let me in and started telling me how the night before she had seen Cederic downtown and they were exchanging CDs. He started hitting on her, and she told him that it would be weird since she used to date my dad. I stood there just taking in all the information.

Cederic's car wasn't across the street, so I knew he wasn't home yet for me to be able to confront the both of them at the same time. Heather walked through the door coming from work. I was in this engrossed conversation with Diane, when Skip Heather's boyfriend proceeded to glorify how good "black pussy" is. I couldn't help thinking to myself that he was just making this whole scenario worse for me. My stomach started turning at the thought of him. He was one apart of the normal crew that would hang out at our house. He was the reason why I was always pretending to be sleep so I wouldn't have to interact with him. Even when I would sleep, he would stand in my bedroom doorway watching me sleep. Goosebumps started rising on all over my body at the thoughts.

Heather turned to me "Why are you in my house?"

"Diane, invited me."

"You need to get out of my house!"

As usual I was problem that she had to get rid of fast. She could see how Skip was staring at me. All I could feel was resentment and anger.

"I don't want him. I'm not like you where I have to take my sister's man because I can't get one."

"You little black bitch," she came charging. Scratching at my face, I just started swinging forgetting all the boxing lessons that I had watched my dad teach people. When she backed away from me, I grabbed one of her wooden chairs and flung it.

"I'm calling the police!"

"Call'um. I don't give a fuck."

I ran outside, pacing in front of her trailer. Racing through my mind, *damn Skip why did you have to say that.* Like you could have been referring to another black woman, seriously. He should have thought that out before he said it. I know he wouldn't like to go to jail behind me for statutory rape. Then the whole town would find out—glorious— because this is exactly how I want people to remember me. I was so wrapped up in my thoughts and pacing in front of Heather's trailer that I didn't see Cederic coming across the street with no shirt on.

"What's going on?"

"What do you mean? What's going on? Why were you hitting on Diane uptown? Don't you know my dad used to date her? Why would you embarrass me like that! Is this funny to you, you think I don't care about you?" Slapping his chest, I saw his skin turning a bright red even at night.

All I wanted to do was cry. I just wanted to cry and lay next to my grandma in bed, crying on her stomach while she would take her hand and run it over my face and through my hair. I could almost smell her, hear her telling me to wipe my tears away because everything was going to be fine. I would just see later, that everything was fine. As quick as the thought came was as quick as it left. I turned back to Cederic.

"How could you do this to me! I don't like Heather, and she doesn't like me. I had to walk over here from home to talk to Diane because of this little stunt you pulled. Now she's calling the police, and I'm going to go jail over you. I wouldn't be here right now if you weren't playing games with my feelings!"

He just stood there realizing the situation that he had caused.

"I'm sorry, I just needed to see."

"See what? What did you need to see, Cederic?"

He grabbed me to stop me from pacing. He pulled me in so close and hugged me.

"I'm so sorry. I just needed to see that you cared for me as much as I cared about you."

When he finished his sentence, Officer Davis pulled up.

"Ms. Clark, do you want to explain to me what's going on here?"

"Yeah, I came over here to talk to Diane and Heather came home. She called me a black bitch and we started fighting."

"Wait here a second. I will be right back."

He went inside the trailer. I could only hear bits of what was being said. One thing was clear, Heather wanted me to go to jail for trespassing in her home. Their voices started getting louder, and I could hear Officer Davis tell her that he couldn't do that, as I was invited onto the premises. He came back out.

"Mr. Martin you need to return home. Ché, you're a long way from home, aren't you?"

"Yes."

"How did you get over here?"

"I walked over here."

"Well, Linda wants you to go to jail."

My heart sunk to the floor.

"But as I explained to her that I would have to take her to jail as well, since you are a minor. So just don't come over to her house anymore, and I'm going to give you a ride home. That was a long walk you took."

"I guess it was," I said, as I pulled the police car door open and sat down.

When I got home, Cederic arrived a few minutes later.

"Ché, I just needed to know that you cared for me like I do you because I want us to get married."

I didn't know what to say at the time. I didn't know what was happening to my life. It seemed like the past summer everything had started to spiral out of control.

Chapter Seven

Within a week, Devin had popped back into our lives, showing up late one night asking for another ride. Cederic was acting like he was sleep, so he wouldn't have to give him a ride, but as usual Devin just asked me.

"Where are you going?"

"Oh, I'm just going up the street, I will give you directions."

"Okay."

I grabbed Cederic's keys and walked out the door. Pulling out of the driveway, he told me to take a right and then less than half a mile down the road another right. There was a dealership right behind our apartments. Devin got out the car and told me to wait. I sat there thinking he was meeting a friend here, or he had lost something. He was looking around on the ground for something. When he grabbed a rock that was as big as a basketball, I just sat there in the car, as if I was watching a movie that I wasn't a part of. He threw the rock into the top part of the door that was glass, reached in and let himself in. I really didn't understand why he needed a ride, especially if his intention was to steal a car. As the screeching of the alarm went off, I sat there in disbelief. I had seen a few things in my few years of age, but watching someone commit a crime with no hesitation as if it is what they were born to do was like a scene out of a movie. He passed me with a bunch of keys in his hands.

"You should probably go," he chuckled at me.

When I got back to the apartment, I woke Cederic up to tell him what happened. Devin was already at the door, and he wanted us to go to Iowa and stash the car there. We followed Devin to give him a ride back to town. When we turned out of town, I saw something being thrown out the window shining from the moonlight. It only took a moment to realize that he had more than a handful of keys to the vehicles and was just throwing them on the side of the road where no one would find them.

Another one of my dad's friends, Lance, appeared later that afternoon, saying that he was meeting up with Devin to get the car. I hadn't seen Lance since my dad started his sentence. I begged Lance to take me with him. I had been cooped up in that apartment with Jodi and I couldn't stand it any longer. He just kept telling me no, that it was best if I stayed at home in case something happened. What he should have said was that he called the police on Devin and that they were going to be waiting for him when they got to Iowa. We wouldn't see Devin for a couple of weeks after this incident because Lance told the police that Devin had guns and rifles that he was supposed to purchase from him. They wouldn't ever find these mysterious guns that seemed to have disappeared in to the air.

I hated seeing my father in jail. Whenever he would go to jail, I usually refused to go see him. We finally went to see him at the beginning of November. We went to the Lancaster's police station. The station was also connected to the jail for the whole County of Grant. We all checked in at the front window while waiting to be called into the visiting area. There was a steel door to the left of the front window and two attached on both sides. An officer came through the door to the right and called out my dad's last name. We walked through the door, passing the officer to six seating areas that were blocked off from each other with two white plastic chairs. I couldn't help but glance to my left and see who was there. Passing the third window, I saw a classmate of mine and gave a surprising wave.

It seemed like it took us 10 minutes to walk the 12 feet to the last window where my dad stood in his County of Grant outfit of white-and-orange striped clothes. He pointed to me that he wanted me to pick up the phone so he could talk to me. I grudgingly picked the phone up.

"What's wrong with you?"

"Nothing." I just kept staring at the ground. He started telling me how the officers were under the impression that me and Cederic were playing the new millennium's Bonnie and Clyde. I turned to Cederic and told him what my father said. Cederic tried to explain that he didn't know what was going on or what he was talking about. Some of the officers were reporting to him what they thought was going on with me. I thought that wasn't too fair since they didn't even have the correct story, but they didn't care about that.

On October 9, 2000, I turned 17 and Cederic dropped off a vase full of roses for me at school. It was the sweetest thing, and actually the only thing that had been done for me in a couple of years. I had usually been left to spend my birthdays alone with no cake or gifts since moving in with my dad. It seemed Grant County also had a gift for me, too. They were charging me with drug trafficking and intent to deliver. They served me the complaint on the evening of my birthday. I thought this was all over. That my dad had did what they wanted and they promised not to do anything to me, but here I was getting served with papers. Devin was eventually released from jail and no sooner than this did he come to my house.

Chapter Eight

A couple of days before November 18, I made an apple streusel cake from scratch. It was for my home economics class because I had missed so much school I had to complete some of my projects at home. This is when I found out that I was allergic to cream of tartar. I had only been eating the cake since there was no food in the house, for the past several days. Then my whole body broke out in welts. The doctor explained to me that if my lips or anything on my face got swollen that I would need to go to the emergency room, as my airways were about to close. Cederic and I had been bouncing between our parents' homes. He thought he would be able to get away from Devin this way but he didn't. The night of November 18, 2000, would be the life-altering change for me. It's the date that I can't seem to escape from, the reason I get so emotional in the fall. It's why I hate the fall.

I began a double dose of Benadryl since my face kept swelling up all that week. I had been spending the majority of my time at Cederic's family's house, while he tried to persuade them to let me move in. Hindsight would have told them to just let me move in and be done with it. We were both better under adult supervision.

When I returned home for the weekend, I thought I was in for a relaxing evening at home. We had went to the video store and rented "The Wood" with Omar Epps, a movie about four black men growing into men and their relationships. I had just taken my medication before Devin knocked on the door.

"What are ya'll doing tonight?"

"You are looking at it," was my reply. "Just drinking and watching movies."

"Why don't we go rob the Pulners' house tonight?"

"Yeah, sure" I said sarcastically. I wasn't in the mood to hear any of his get-rich quick schemes. The visit with my dad showed me how things were getting around town that everything was my fault, when in reality, I didn't have a premeditated knowledge of what was going on.

"I'm serious! Why don't we go? I mean we could get enough money and just split town. Well, you can take the money and I will take the drugs. Does that sound about even?"

"Sure Devin, whatever you say," I said sarcastically. Cederic hadn't said a word. He was probably thinking about his own problems.

Today was his first day on probation for a crime he had no involvement in. My dad was the drug dealer of the town, but he didn't compare to the drug system that the Pulners ran. Earlier that summer, three of my dad's associates came over gloating about how they had robbed the Pulners' house for $50,000 and split the money between them. They laughed at how dumb Cederic was because he didn't know that they were robbing the house, but he was the one that got stuck paying the majority of that money back even though they didn't share a dime with him.

I had finished my first couple of beers as this conversation continued. Devin just wouldn't leave it alone.

"I mean you got that drug case, and we could just get enough money to split town and be done with this place. I wouldn't have to worry about any of my cases either. We could go to Mexico."

"I can't do that. I just can't leave like that." I couldn't tell him that I was too scared to leave. That I had tried to run away before and it didn't work out. That if I ran, my dad would find me and he would kill me. Children make this statement all the time, but I was one of them who knew to take that statement literally. I was going to graduate in a year. I don't know who glorified being on the run for the rest of your life, but I didn't want to live the rest of my life paranoid that Leon was going to come after me one day or that I could get pulled over for a traffic ticket and be found out years later.

"Man, come on. We should just do it."

"What are we supposed to do if someone is there?"

"Don't worry about that. I will take care of that. I mean we can just kill them if we have to.

Jodi had been in the corner just listening to the whole conversation. "Well I don't know about the killing part but it doesn't seem like a bad idea to me. We could catch up on rent and the other bills."

I couldn't believe her at any other time she didn't have anything to say, and now all of a sudden she had something to say when it included doing something illegal! I just hated this woman with every fiber in my body. I just wondered how she could sit back and watch my dad do everything he did to me. Why didn't she ever help me? I could still taste her in my mouth sometimes and it made me want to throw up. I hated her and blamed her for everything; all of this was her fault. How did she even meet my dad? Why did she move up here to work at a minimum wage job? I didn't get it. It wasn't like he would kill her. He had her empty out her 401k, whatever that is. I didn't care, I just didn't want her in my face.

I started feeling the buzz as I looked over at my medication box realizing that I wasn't supposed to drink with it. I wanted to go to sleep. I needed to lie down. I hadn't ever gotten this drunk off of a six pack. Devin wanted to talk about robbing the Pulners' house. I got up and made it to my bedroom before I started dozing off in the midst of his conversation.

When I woke up, Devin was on top of me, the light was on and Cederic was screaming. I didn't get what was going on. It didn't take a scientist to put together that Devin took his opportunity to get what he wanted from me. Cederic was flipping out; he was completely red. I didn't know what to do.

"We're playing around. He isn't even doing anything."

"Then why doesn't he have his pants on, Ché?" *What the hell am I going to do here?* I hadn't fully understood what was going on, I just wanted to calm Cederic down. Instead of assessing the situation, I decided to fly off the handle, too. I ran after him down the hall, realizing that I was wearing only a tee shirt. He had already reached the front door. We were just screaming, as I reached for the cabinets. I threw every dish we had, breaking almost every dish we had. Devin came from the back hall.

"You should get in the shower so you can sober up a little. You're fucked up."

"Yeah, sure."

"Here put these black pants on. You can wear my hoodie. Cederic, come on. All you have to do is drive. That's it."

Jodi piped in, "Cederic, come on. All you have to do is drive. It is no big deal. You're just driving."

I don't know how it was done, but we were all in the car driving down the main street.

Devin kept telling us this elaborate plan to go to Madison when we had everything. When we got to the main highway, Cederic saw Officer Cop driving towards us. Cederic started panicking, "That's Officer Cop," he was imitating an asthma attack. How Devin calmed him down I'm not sure, but we ended up at the gas station. Cederic was going to leave Devin there, if only he had the heart to pull off.

When Devin came back, we went to the Pulners' house. We had pulled along a side street and parked. Devin started rushing us.

"Hurry! Come on, let's go!."

"I really don't think we should do this. Ché, please don't do this."

All I heard was a deep thud, as Devin punched deep into his chest. Cederic stopped objecting. I just sat there slouched in the back seat. I still hadn't sobered up. I just didn't want to fight anymore.

"I'll go in the house. Ché can drive."

Cederic thought this was the best plan with me in the state I was in. This should have been my clue, but for someone who was inebriated, it wasn't a clue, it was an order.

"Ché is coming in the house with me. It has to be Ché."

"I don't get it," Cederic said. "Why can't I just go with you?" Another deep thud sounded off in the car.

"Okay...okay. I'm getting out of the car." I slipped out of the car and tried to gain my footing.

I didn't even know which house it was, so I just followed Devin down the slope of someone's backyard. It was the third house down right in the middle. There were concrete side stairs that led to the back door. Devin pulled the wire cutters out of his backpack.

"I'm going to cut the lines so no one can call the police. Here you carry the bat and the bag."

I was sitting there when my stomach started hurting. I couldn't gather if it was from the beer or that I didn't have a good feeling about this at all. Devin came back from the side of the house after he cut the wires and reached for the screen door. I started praying that it would be locked and could just go back to the car or maybe the door would be locked. It wasn't. Devin went into the house first and when he was half way in the door, he grabbed my hand and led me into the kitchen. It wasn't as dark as if people were sleeping and my eyes adjusted very quickly from the light seeping from the TV and upstairs hall. There was a glass armoire to my left next to the back door that reached the ceiling. Devin walked into the house like he was at home. I was stuck in my shoes like they were glued to the floor. *What am I doing, what is going on?* I still couldn't move. As Devin took another step toward the living room, I started to inch towards the door watching Devin enter the living room. I slid my back along the wall toward the door, watching him to make sure he didn't see that I was inching out of the house. When he called my name, I had the door open.

I couldn't do this! What was I thinking! How did I even get here? Then I heard rustling, "Freeze!"

I was half way out of the door, but my body got slammed in the doorway from someone trying to open the basement door.

"Hey, it's me. I'm the one that called you guys." I could hear Devin screaming. I leaped off the porch not touching a stair. Everything dropped from my hands suddenly as the adrenaline had kicked in and I wasn't drunk anymore. I was well aware of what had just happened. I just needed to make it to the car. I thought, *we will be safe as long as I make it to the car.* I ran right into the car and bounced off. My depth perception was obviously still off. I jumped in the car, screaming "Go!" Cederic asked where Devin was, and all I could do was scream, "He is still in the house! The police are in the house! He set us up! What are we going to do"

"We're just going to go back to your house like we never left, that's it. We don't know nothing." His face turned gray like he wanted to believe everything that he just said. We parked on the side street to my house and ran to the apartment, breaking through the branches.

Once we were back in the house, Jodi wanted to know what happened. I had already changed into some pajamas.

"Jodi just don't say anything. We were here the whole night. No one saw me." My mind was just frantic. Cederic and I went to lie down. After lying next to each for about 10 minutes, I thought it was over. That this cruel joke was over, until I heard the gravel crunching under tires coming into the driveway. I could hear Jodi telling the police that we were in the back asleep.

The light came on. "Mr. North, hands above your head." Cederic was gone in a flash. I just stood there staring at the ground saying that we were home all night. They cuffed me in the middle of the hall in my pajama tee-shirt. I couldn't believe this Officer Cop came from the back and helped me put some pants on and sat me on the couch. Jodi kept telling them that we were there all night until they put the cuffs on. The police knew exactly what to say to her.

"What do you think B is going to say if you go to jail"

She burst out, "I don't know where they went, but they left a little bit ago." I just turned and glared at her. This was all her fucking fault in the first place, this fucking bitch. I didn't even say anything else. I was too tired. I went to sleep on the 10-minute ride to the county jail in Lancaster.

I was booked, and they lead me down to cell block C. It was in the middle of the night, so I just went into the first cell, as they closed the barred door, I laid on the inch-thick mattress and went to sleep. I woke up the next morning when they called us for breakfast. I wasn't hungry. I was in jail. I kept going over that whole night in my mind. Officer Cop came to talk to me that day and get a statement. I knew how this worked (right?). I would just give them something that they wanted and they would let me go. I had a long conversation with him before he went and got the tape recorder. He didn't even have it with him the first 20 minutes that we talked. He promised me that I would get out on Monday on a signature bond if I just admitted to doing everything. What possessed me to believe him was the hope that for once in my life someone actually cared and wouldn't lie to me. He proved me wrong.

"What do you want? Do you want Lance? Devin?"

"Oh, no, Ché. I'm going to need something big in order to get you out. Do you know where the guns are?"

"What guns?" I was already lost in this conversation.

"Oh, you know the guns you and Devin stole from Muscoda"

"I don't know what you are talking about."

He just kept staring at me, "Well what do you have for me?" His eyes lit up like the next words out of my mouth were going to give him an honorary award for all his hard work. My eyes turned dark and I stared at him. I knew what he wanted, he wanted my dad. He wanted me to give him my dad on a platter, like a roasted pig for Thanksgiving dinner. *Never.* We were having this full conversation with our eyes for a couple of minutes.

"I have nothing else I can give."

"Well, then I guess you will just be sitting here then."

"They already let Jodi go. Cederic has a probation violation now so he won't get out for a while. You know that was his first day on probation for robbing that same house?" He started chuckling at the stupidity of it all. My heart fell straight to the freezing floor. *How fair is this to him?* I made my choice that it wasn't fair for him, and I made my statement.

Trying to make it seem like he didn't know anything was going on. I just didn't know what to say.

"I don't know what to say."

"How about this? I will go get the tape recorder and you can answer as we go along."

My mind searched for ways to make everything my fault, while I waited for him to come back into the conference room with the tape recorder. I just didn't want Cederic to get in trouble behind me. All he wanted was me, and this is what he gets? Officer Cop came back with the recorder. I started making the statement before I realized it I had started crying on the tape at my attempt to be a responsible adult.

"Is there anything else you have to say?"

I had paused to mouth to him if he was going to let me out, and he shook his head *yes*, and I just started to cry all over again. Trying to find some rational reasoning of why I was at that house. I couldn't. All I could say was that I needed to pay the bills, which came out with me saying the cable bill was due.

After I made the statement, I went back to the cell. Tessa came over to introduce herself and Tina just stayed in her cell. They were both serving time for drug charges. Tina lived in a suburb outside of Chicago and was pulled over for a traffic ticket in Wisconsin. Almost six years ago, she had a drug case that she fled from and now it was time for her to pay the piper. Tessa was serving a probation sentence. She was originally on probation for selling drugs and then was caught while on probation selling drugs to an informant. They were both serving six months for their crimes and had commenced their sentence together. Tessa asked me why I was there, and I explained that I had been set up by Devin, after he had come up with a plan to do everything.

Chapter Nine

Before I went to court on Monday morning, I finally decided that maybe I should I call my grandmother and mom to see if they might be able to help me. It was clear from our conversation that I shouldn't say anything to anybody, but I had already made that mistake.

"Ché? What's going on?"

"I'm in jail Grandma."

"What happened? You know what don't say anything, just don't say anything at all. Does it have to do with drugs?"

"No."

"Don't worry we're going to get you out of there? I knew something like this was going to end up happening. Are there other women in there?"

"Yeah."

"Well don't say anything to them. Remember, Ché, don't tell them anything at all."

It was difficult having a conversation about your roommates with them sitting right next to you. Cell block C was a rectangular shaped cell; there were three separate cells that had metal barred doors that closed at night. The outer area was the length of all the three 10 x 8 cells and 10 feet wide. There was a shower that was on the opposite side of the wall that was open so everyone could see you showering. This would be the first and last time that I would give any information out about my case.

The jail was so over packed that there were men across the hall in the women's sections of the jail in cell block D. Cederic just so happened to be across the hall. He went to court that morning. When he returned he warned me that night that my roommate had told on me and not to say anything else. Tina had told me when I came back from court that I should not say anything else concerning my case. I asked her where Tessa had disappeared to. Tina told me she was called out as soon as I left for court and that's all she knew. As soon as Tessa came back, I was moved immediately. It still hadn't sunk in exactly what happened. I was by myself for a couple of days and then Candy came. She was 17, too. The guard explained that because we were minors, we couldn't be with the adults, even if we were being charged as adults. I would watch many roommates come and go, my weekend warrior, Tina, Shawn, Sue, Jess, Sara, Tera, Melissa, and Amy.

It wasn't enough for Tessa to make a bogus statement on me, but she also told everyone that I stunk. Every time I got a new roommate, the first thing they would say to me was how I didn't stink like she said I did. I wouldn't get the full statement that Tessa gave to Office Cop until it got closer to trial but the damage had already been done.

After Candy finished her 20 days, she left, and Sara moved in my cell. She was really quiet and understood the loyalty of family. She was seven months pregnant when one of her brothers took her car and filled the gas tank up and drove off. She knew if she turned him in that he would go to prison for his actions so she decided to sit the 30 days out instead of turning him in. She would later return for check forgery. She didn't have all the items that she wanted for her newborn and wrote a check that she knew wouldn't cover. She planned it out perfectly; she would pay for the items by spending the 30 days in jail. We would play card games all day. It had been a couple of months since I had been in jail when her pregnancy made me realize that I hadn't gotten my period. I told her then I might be pregnant and also told my GED tutor Henry.

Henry was a very nice man. He treated me like I was still human. After he discovered that I was ready to test out for my GED, we would just sit and talk. For once, I felt like someone was actually listening to me and trying to understand what was going on in my life. I told Henry everything how my mom didn't want me living with her anymore when I was 11. How my dad had gotten stuck in Wisconsin because he was called a racial slur by a police officer who had pulled him over. He assaulted the officer, and after he was released, he was just deserted to the town we were living in now. I explained how I was bouncing between my grandmother's house to my mother's. How my mom made me call my grandmother and see if I could stay with her. How my grandmother said that it wasn't her responsibility every time my mom had a problem with me and that she couldn't just keep throwing me off on people. And that's how I ended up with my dad.

I remembered it like it was yesterday. I told him how I tried to kill myself by drinking bleach that summer when I was 11 after our neighbor across the street tried to rape me. How my mom did nothing, letting him grope me in front of her, and then she would call me a whore. He would just sit and listen to all of it nodding as we would go along. He explained that my mom was making me the parent in the home at an early age. After a few tell-all sessions, he finally asked me, "I can't believe that with everything that you have been through, why you haven't already been in trouble. Why aren't you a delinquent?"

My head bowed to the table. *How was I supposed to answer that question?*

"That's just not who I am. I'm a good person. Because that's not how "the best little girl in the world would act." My eyes started tearing up.

"I'm sorry I didn't mean it like that. It just seems like for as young as you are you have been through quite a few hardships already."

The last time we met, he had some news for me. "I think there's something you might find interesting."

"What's that?"

"Devin made the news. It seems he beat some guy into a coma in front of the grocery store in Lancaster!"

I couldn't believe it. I just knew that I was going to get out then. If they let him out, they would have to let me go since he was out there beating people to death almost.

"Was it just him?" I said, trying to assess the situation better.

"No, it wasn't. There were a couple of them. I don't think he is going to be able to beat this case. There were several witnesses."

The next outing, I had out of my cell was with a social worker. She only had a few questions concerning school. It had already been several months since I had been incarcerated. I started becoming very resentful, and I just kept staring at her with her dark curly hair. I finally broke the silence, "Where were you months ago?"

"Excuse me?"

"I don't get it. Why did you even let me go back to that house when I got caught with the drugs?"

"Well, your case is just now hitting my desk."

"Like six months later?"

"I can't help it when I get the cases."

I had nothing to say to her after that. She just kept asking me about school. Oh, I get it the school administrators were trying to cover themselves now and say that I was truant, how convenient. The only times I would leave my cell from this point on would be to move in between the cells and for court.

Before Sara finished her sentence, I took a pregnancy test that was negative. She told me that she wasn't a doctor, but she thought the test was wrong. She had been watching me the last couple of weeks and I was showing signs of an early pregnancy. After she left and I was by myself, it happened again. I got the worse cramps of my life. All I could do was lie on the mattress and ball up. I was bleeding through everything. I was bleeding so horrendously. I couldn't comprehend what was going on. I decided to get in the shower, but the cramping just wouldn't stop. I stood in the shower with the little sprayer washing over me, crying. It didn't take a scientist to figure out what was happening. I couldn't stop crying, or bleeding. I looked down and there was a blood clot bigger than my hand lying on the bottom of the concrete shower. I just cried, cried for the baby that I would never have. Cried because they lied to me and told me that I wasn't pregnant. I didn't understand how they even knew to test me. It wouldn't be until after I was found guilty that I would finally figure out that they had been listening through the intercom to me every day.

Chapter Ten

My dad was released in February. After he got out, I got his TV. This helped me keep my mind off everything. The day before, I had just gone to court and it was decided that I should go to trial first. My lawyer looked at me and told me that it was only going to get worse if that's what happened.

"Ché, I'm sorry to tell you this, but they are leading the black sheep to be slaughtered. It isn't the best idea in our situation, but there isn't anything that we can do about it."

Our case was based on Devin intimidating Cederic, and if he didn't go to trial first, he was more than likely not going to testify at mine. I started losing myself in the cell by myself. Watching the same TV series over and over was the only way to know what time of day it was. Not knowing what was going on with my schoolmates or Cederic, the miscarriage, and now going to trial. It was too much for me. I didn't want to be. I didn't want any part of my life any more. Nothing else mattered to me.

I concocted a plan. I could request a razor any time that the guards came down the hall to check on me. We all knew that Cari, one of the guards, was ready to retire and extremely forgetful. She came around to give us razors to shave, but she forgot to pick mine up as I knew she would. I waited until she dropped off lunch, knowing she wouldn't be back for a couple of hours until dinnertime. I kept thinking that if I did it right, it would only take a couple of minutes.

I started carving away at my wrist. The little flimsy razor just wouldn't cut deep enough. It wasn't like in the movies when you would see someone make a clean cut and the blood streams out like a river bursting through a dam. I kept carving away at my wrist, slashing and trying to make the razor cut deeper until I heard the crackle over the intercom announcing I had a visitor and to get ready. I dropped the razor. I could hear Cari's voice crackling over the intercom, "Ché, you have a visitor, so get ready."

Who was here to see me? I tried covering my arm by putting on a plain-gray sweatshirt handed out during the winter, with the sleeves so no one would notice my poor attempt to kill myself.

The visiting room for women only had two seats. I walked in looking across the glass at Binky. Then I saw Tessa's thick black hair. All I could feel was anger. I looked over and there was my dad. He looked sick; there was no color in his face. He asked me what I had been up to and I showed him my arm. He tried to console me and make me feel like it would be okay, but I knew that it wasn't. I spent the rest of our visit screaming about how Tessa snitched on me. *Why would they put me in a visiting room alone with her?* My dad just explained that I needed to calm down. I didn't want to calm down; I wanted to ruin her visit. I wanted to ruin her life for lying on me and telling people that I stink.

Mission accomplished. When we were walking back to our cells, I could hear her mocking my screaming and how it ruined her visit. Cari asked me if I needed anything. I was still overwhelmed with hatred.

"Yeah, make me blonde with blue eyes, because if I was, this shit wouldn't be happening to me and I would be out of here! How is it okay to let someone out who beat another person into a coma yet I have to sit in here and rot?" Luckily for me, I would encounter Beth again before court. This time, I wouldn't go ballistic.

In March, the jail was so full that all the women were in a five-person cell, and three of us were on the floor. The men had outgrown their quarters and used the two other blocks on the women's wing. One of the women on the floor with me was waiting to go to court for her first arraignment and she was really worried. When Tessa found out I had court before Sam, she told her it would be fine, that she was going to court in between a murderess and a prostitute and they would let her out on her petty crime. She called me a murderess all night, taunting me, wanting me to react to her. Finally, Sue and Shawn got tired of hearing her remarks and told her to shut up. She didn't say another word to me. I knew that if I said anything that could be considered threatening, it would be taken as that. I just chose not to speak. I knew what the consequences of my actions would have been at this point. I would be assigned another charge and be in the position where no one would believe me again.

Chapter Eleven

I told my lawyer the very next morning that they kept putting me in a cell with Tessa and that she would go through my papers as she was known to do. We were separated immediately. I felt like they were just trying to provoke me into more charges. We got moved out of the women's section to the middle. The jail was a long rectangle. On one side was the women's block and the other end had the men's section. But there was a cell block right in the middle next to the control station and that's where we were put. Jen seemed very upset about the whole situation. She was the type of guard who didn't show emotion, and she didn't side with the officers, but she didn't side with us either.

She treated her job with respect and followed the protocols. She was flustered while she explained to us that I was moving to E and it was a four-person cell. She had already pulled Tessa out of the cell. She asked who wanted to move with me. Sue, Shawn, and Michael would be my new roommates for a little bit. At first, we were all quiet, but then the silence was broken when Shawn realized I was B's daughter. Her boyfriend Paul had also been from Columbus and they had met my dad. I went to school with her daughter, and that's when everything sunk in for her.

It would seem that I had gained two new adoptive parents with this new arrangement. Sue was part Native American and felt that she was being discriminated against with her case. She was waiting to see what was going to happen to her. She was on probation in a county four hours north of here. None us of understood why she was all the way in Grant County. She explained that her case originated from Grant County, so even though she didn't live here anymore, she would always have to come back here to have her case looked at. I thought that was the most ridiculous waste of taxpayers' money. Just the transportation alone was hundreds of dollars! She explained that she decided to take a day off of work and her probation officer happened to call her job that day. Because she didn't tell her officer that she took a day off, her officer had her turn herself into the jail so she could meet with her. Sue waited a week before her officer came to see her, and she was fired from her job because she had missed a whole week of work. When her officer found out that she got fired, she felt Sue was not completing the conditions of her probation. This put Sue back in jail and now she had to sit the rest of her sentence, which was supposed to be probation, in jail.

Shawn was there for writing bad checks. Her husband should have paid them off, but she said it would have been a waste of money. She would just sit her time out and they could use that money to go on vacation.

Once we were all acquainted, they started telling me all the nasty things that Tessa was saying, and that they were glad that they got to know me. My court dates were coming faster and faster. I pleaded guilty to the juvenile drug charge because the district attorney wanted to charge me as an adult. The judge decided not to sentence me because he was overseeing my other charges. Saying that the adult punishment for the adult charges would probably precede anything, they would sentence me in juvenile court. It seemed as soon as I pleaded guilty, then all the other court dates fell into place. The motion hearing took place, then the next week we would pick the jurors, and then the pre-trial would start. I would not face a jury of my peers. Shawn and Sue felt that I should have my case moved out of the county since it was so high-profile for the area where I lived. When I finally followed their advice, it was too late.

My lawyer explained that we had already had our motion hearing and we should have presented the request at that time. We were headed for trial. Before the trial, my lawyer called me and explained that they had put a plea on the table. Jen passed the phone through the tray hole so I could speak with him.

"I'm going to tell you, Ché, I think this is a horrible deal, but I have to let you know, okay? What's on the table is they are willing to plea bargain for: 30 years in prison and 45 years on probation." Wisconsin had just passed its Truth in Sentencing Law, which meant that there was no more good time. If you were sentenced to 10 years, then you completed 10 years.

Thank goodness I had a support system. I had reached the point where anything sounded good just as long as I knew about it. Sitting for the past seven months just wondering what was going to happen had driven me to my wits' end. Shawn talked me out of the plea very quickly. A couple of days before trial, they put another plea bargain: 15 years in prison and 30 years on probation. This plea was rejected as well. Shawn still couldn't understand why we couldn't move the case to a different county since it was so high profile in Grant County, and there would be no minorities on my jury.

Every time I went to court, it was like a circus. When we started picking the jurors, all of them knew of the case.

They either read about it in the newspaper, or heard it from a friend and discussed it over a drink at the bar. I thought a woman in the first row looked familiar, but I just brushed it off. Suddenly, she jumped up and explained that I was her daughter's best friend and she couldn't do it.

I had previously been to school with her daughter in Lancaster for a semester because my high school had discontinued our French-language courses. Watching her break down on the bench made me feel like something was wrong; maybe this was more serious than I was taking it. I had been listening to everyone tell me what was wrong and what was right, never stopping to ask myself the difference. It wasn't right that the case was built on hearsay or entrapment. No one could even understand why I hadn't been released, why I was still sitting in jail waiting to go to trial, with a $50,000.00 bond. Our families kept encouraging us that things were going to be okay. This was the first time that our actions from that night sank in. Our classmates thought it was a huge joke. Everyone was in disbelief.

The jurors were finally picked, and my lawyer said that it seemed half and half, but he really wanted to get more women because they were more sympathetic. I had no idea how this was going to go. I would just sit at the table like an emotionless doll staring into the wall and looking out the window at my first glimpse of sunshine. When they brought my dad out in his prison uniform as a character witness, Mr.

Hines, my lawyer, was furious as he knew the damage that was cause among the jury. He had explained that during trials, everyone was supposed to be given street clothes if they are incarcerated, so that the jury doesn't know that the witness is incarcerated. Even though Dad was a witness, he explained that he was not allowed by the sheriffs to change into street clothes. My lawyer was very upset by this. I had held my composure until this point. No one could understand that the breakdown of the tears falling over my fat cheeks and blubbering of snot out my nose wasn't because I loved my dad so much, but rather that I couldn't bear to see him in that situation.

It was the fact that when he was taken away long ago, I felt like that abandoned little girl, that little girl in a little blue-jean dress being dragged outside of another prison's visitors' room not understanding why my father was chained from head to toe. I was screaming and unable to understand why I couldn't be with him. *Why was he so far away?*

Seeing him in that prison outfit brought back that three-year-old girl kicking and screaming and throwing a fit in the prison entry way. I wouldn't cry again during the rest of my court appearances, not even at my sentencing. My family was behind me supporting me and giving me words of encouragement. My grandmother and mother, along with my oldest younger brother, had come to see me through my trial. One of the women that I was incarcerated with, my weekend warrior's sister, showed up. During one of our breaks, I turned to my mom as the judge was passing us.

"Mom, I think I'm going to miss the prom."

"Ché, you have more serious matters to think about right now than whether or not you are going to be able to go to the prom."

I don't know why I thought I was going to walk away from this situation unscathed.

I took the stand on the first day of trial. I can still remember testifying and this woman with glasses with a short brunette bob asking me if we had stopped at the gas station, why hadn't I just jumped out of the car.

"I couldn't just leave Cederic. I loved him."

They waited for Devin to take the stand last. It had been months since I had seen him. The last time I saw him was a couple of months ago when he went on trial for all the burglaries we had supposedly committed together. I told the district attorney then that I didn't want to testify against him because I was scared. He didn't believe me, nor did the jurors, even though I gave them every detail they needed to convict him, but it was as plain as a sunny day that my words fell on deaf ears. My chest started heaving in anger. I wanted to scream to the top of my lungs that he was a bastard. *How could he do this to me?* I didn't want to be like him all drugged out and waiting for the next hit. Didn't he understand that I was supposed to go to college and do something with my life? He created all this misery in my life even though he said he loved me. Is this what you do to the person that you want to marry, because I didn't get that memo? No, this isn't what you do to the person you want to marry. Yet his personality spoke for itself. He would steal from his mother and grandmother relentlessly. He was a drug addict, the type of person that was used to getting everything that he wanted. He couldn't understand why I didn't pick him. For him, I was unattainable, so why would he care?

Devin was refusing to testify in my case, telling his story of how he was supposed to get off of all the charges he had open and hadn't. The assistant district attorney and the judge threatened him with perjury. He said it didn't matter to him. With all the charges he had, taking the perjury felon charge was a minor sentence for him compared to all his open cases. It was in that moment that I had a little glimmer of hope and he would tell the jury his devious plan to entrap me. But what he told the jury was that I was drunk beyond comprehension, which was very true. I could see that he was getting upset because of whatever deal he had struck with them he didn't believe was going to help him at this stage. If he testified, then he would still be held accountable for all his other crimes.

Cederic came out next to say that he was pleading the Fifth Amendment, so it all boiled down to my word against Devin. Jodi never took the stand. I couldn't understand why she wasn't taking the stand, as she was there that night. My lawyer later explained that she agreed not to testify on my behalf if they didn't charge her with contributing to a minor because she bought the alcohol that night. I was completely disgusted that Cederic was leaving me to be fed to the wolves. I didn't have a jury of my peers at all, which is why the case should have been moved out of that county. I thought that we all had a right to a fair trial, which this wasn't turning out to be. The only thing good I did have on my side was Devin's mother taking the stand and telling the jury how Devin was a pathological liar. I thought to myself that I was going to be fine. They would believe me, as all they wanted was the truth, right? No matter how you looked at it, no matter right was right and wrong was wrong, my whole case was built on the fact that he coerced us to commit a crime that he had planned.

Chapter Twelve

After all the testimonies and the closing arguments, the sheriffs drove me back to the jail and placed me in a holding cell until they got the call to bring me back. The jury had deliberated for a couple of hours. Right before their verdict came, they gave me another plea: eight years in prison and 15 years of extended supervision. My mother was like "No, they have nothing, and they are not going to find you guilty." That's what we all thought. Standing and listening to the verdict, I couldn't believe my ears.

"We the jury find the defendant, Ché Clark, on the count of conspiracy to reckless endangerment, guilty; for the count of damage of property, not guilty; and for the count of burglary guilty."

My face fell in astonishment. *What did I expect?* Did I honestly really think that the people who were supposed to care about and take care of me would stand up for me? Did I honestly think that for once someone would come save me from this horror? This was just another chapter to add to this horrific life that I was leading. I stood there emotionless and when I started to quiver, while my father's threats rang in my ears: *I hate when you listen to this soft shit, that's why you are weak! Who the fuck is the white bitch, Jewel? Get this sensitive as shit out my face. Don't you know whose daughter you are?* I could hear his voice inside my head like he was right there next to my face, his alcohol breath smothering me while I was cowering in the corner. I would be emotionless until they let me go back to my cell.

As soon as I heard the metal door close behind me, my statue-like shock broke. I stood motionless, crying where I stood. I tried explaining to everyone that they found me guilty, but they could barely understand me. Shawn and Sue were right there for me coming to my side and guiding me the three feet to my metal bed, while trying to calm me down. I sat on the edge of my metal bed crying in disbelief that my life was over. They couldn't believe the verdict either. We tried to focus on anything but my sentencing date. I finally mustered up the courage to call Cederic's family to see what their reaction was. They hadn't come to my trial. The only person from his family who came was his Aunt Pam. His sister picked up the phone and proceeded to tell me that they told him to take the plea bargain the district attorney gave him after I was convicted. He took a plea agreement for five years for his probation violation and two-and-a-half years for our case totaling seven-and-a-half years in prison and two-and-a-half years on extended supervision. I couldn't believe that they gave him that much time. I just didn't understand. His sister tried calming me down, but that wasn't going to work at this point. I just knew that I was going to get double the time that Cederic got.

During the pre-sentence investigation, Todd was my investigator. He told me over the phone that my family was scared that I was going to try to kill myself while I was there. They didn't know that I had already tried, that when I was 11 I drank half a bottle of bleach because I wanted to die. He thought everything was for show.

"Ché, with all that you have been through in your life, I don't understand why you are not on crack somewhere whoring yourself."

I was so disgusted with how he was talking to me. I couldn't make the right words to come out, except, "that's just not the person that I am."

"Well anyway, I'm going to recommend that you go to prison for seven years and 10 on extended supervision."

My little world was getting smaller and smaller. I couldn't grasp everything that was happening. I started crying in my sleep.

A week before the sentencing court date, we were all sitting around listening to the radio when Sam was pulled out of the cell. As soon as she was pulled out, the radio went off. We kept busy talking and giggling like we were at a huge slumber party. Everyone's time started dwindling down and would leave within the next 30 days. Sam came back after a little while. I was sitting on Shawn's bed watching her play a card game that Sue had finally talked her into.

Sam burst into tears, "It's going to be all my fault if you go to prison!"

Everyone turned to her confused.

"What are you talking about," Shawn spouted.

By this time I had turned to Sam, face to face. Her eyes had already started swelling up because she was crying so hard.

"I'm so sorry Ché. I'm so sorry if you go to prison. It's going to be my fault."

"It's not going to be anyone's fault but my own. I shouldn't have gone to that woman's house drunk or not. I just don't understand how a criminal trespassing turns into burglary and conspiracy to reckless injury because a pathological liar says so."

Sue piped in, "Wait a minute. You were drunk when you committed the crime right?"

"Yeah, that's a fact."

"Did they ever test your alcohol limit when they brought you in?"

"No."

"See, Ché, I hate to say this, but I don't think it would have mattered if you stayed at your house. They were out to get you no matter what. They would have tried to pin something on you." Sue didn't get a chance to finish her last sentence as one of the guards came in and moved Sam.

We all knew then that with her emotional breakdown and guilt-stricken face that she had given the police a statement. I told everyone that there wasn't anything that she could've said that would hurt me, except a lie. The three burglaries that Devin had committed weren't solved and he was acquitted of all charges. Sam signed a typed letter stating that I told her I did it, and that I had this private conversation with her in the bathroom. The statement made me sound like this devious little minion of my father's. When everyone found out, they couldn't believe the lengths that the police were going to convict me. The burglary charges that I had testified about at Devin's trial, I was now being charged with. Burglary, perjury (accusing Devin of rape) which he was never charged with, and armed robbery. I couldn't believe it; all that I could hear was the voice of the Muscoda officer telling me that I would take the blame for everything and I didn't listen.

During my sentencing, my grandmother had brought a lawyer with her and he took the stand to propose that I be sent to the Teen Challenge of her state because of my age. My grandmother also took the stand and explained that what I had done was not in my character. She would have understood if it involved drugs, but this was just ludicrous. The judge didn't even consider sending me to Teen Challenge; I guess he thought sending a 17-year-old who didn't even really know her own body would be better off with a pack of manipulating, abused women.

"Ché, I'm doing this to get you away from all the B's, Devins, and Cederics in your life. That's why I'm sentencing you to two-and-a-half years in prison and seven-and-a-half on probation."

He could have sent me to Teen Challenge as well and I would have been away from them! If they care so much about moving me away from these types of people, why didn't they take me out of my father's custody during the first raid! All I could feel was the hatred for this neglectful system that led me down this path of expecting different results. I had sat in jail now for eight months wasting my life watching sitcoms all day and doing absolutely nothing. Shawn was released to a different county to serve out her time there, and Sue was right behind her. The next day, I left.

Chapter Thirteen

It was a three-hour ride to Dodge Correctional with my wrists shackled to another chain to the shackles around my feet. I was riding with two men; one was trying to frighten me and the other Terry was trying to give me the ropes. They were both astonished at my age. One of them had read about my case in the newspaper taunting me by calling me a murderess and the mastermind behind it all. Both of them had been through the intake process before. Terry finally calmed me down and tried to explain things to me in a way so that I wouldn't be so frightened. He tried to explain what would happen once we left that vehicle.

First, we would be separated so I wouldn't see them ever again and get the chance to thank him for not making the situation more humiliating for me. Then I would go through a process called intake. As the car rolled up to the prison, I couldn't fathom its size. We parked in a garage that looked like a shipping docking area. They headed to the left and I went to the right. As soon as I walked in, there was a small hall where a woman guard met us. The hall was only a few feet long before it opened up into a wide area.

The first order of business was a shower that's surrounded in cement with a metal button in the middle of the wall to push for the water. There was about four of them lined up to the left and wide open so I could see the women ahead of me showering and a women guard would be right across from them watching for any contraband. First, I stripped my clothes off, lifted one breast then the other, squatted and coughed, turned around and did it again, and then I was given lice shampoo to put on all the hairy parts of my body. Then I got a set of dark evergreen prison uniforms that smelled of starch and body odors and a used sports bra that had the name of the institution stamped on the back of it.

Once I had ridded my body of any lice and was clean, I walked around the corner into another hall. Then I took a left and went down another hall, where I stood in a long line of 20 or so women getting their pictures taken for their identification card with their inmate number. In a little open room, I saw the men who are completing their intake passing on the opposite wall.

After this "lovely" ride, I was sent upstairs with the rest of the women who had been sent there like me. Walking down this corridor the floors were so cold I felt it through my little slip-on shoes. All the women who just arrived were sent to stay on the third floor. I would have to stay on the third floor until I was cleared of TB, or any other medical conditions. I was also swabbed so that the state of Wisconsin now has my DNA for any other crimes I might commit or have previously committed but haven't been convicted yet.

Soon, I was at my cell with a metal toilet that has a little sink attached to it. I knew these toilets hurt during the wintertime from the previous winter I spent in jail. So I was thankful that I was there around summer.

During the first seven days, I was not allowed to leave my cell at all. My meals were brought to my cell. This is when they did all their medical testing as well. Dodge Correctional was just an intake prison. I was there for around a month to be assessed. Once they reviewed my case, they decided where to send me and what institution would be best for me. There were only three women's prisons. Taycheedah was a maximum/medium prison. If I or anyone else had more than five years to serve, needed drug counseling, or had open cases like I did, we were sent there.

Since I had open cases and I had committed my crime while I was under the influence, I had to complete alcohol and other drugs assessment (AODA). They gave me a list of things that they recommended that I do while I was there like getting a high school diploma, or completing drug treatment. Being stuck in a cell with another person all day would drive me crazy, especially if we don't get along.

Chapter Fourteen

My first roommate moved the day I came in before I could even catch her name. Celia was my second roommate. She had curves in all the right places, and her skin was so dark and beautifully clear. I had never seen someone so dark and sexy. She was bright and always had a smile on her face. I hadn't met anyone dark-skinned who was so beautiful, which was refreshing for me since I grew up feeling that I was ugly because I had dark skin. If you asked her why she was there, she would tell you that it was drug-related and that was it. I guess since we had no interaction really with the outside world this is what we were left with, finding out each other's issues and stories. I didn't know what to do in prison.

Celia had gone through her previous roommate's court papers. Her roommate had killed her abusive boyfriend and was sentenced to only 18 months. They both went to the hole for arguing and Celia became my roommate after that. So I just decided to tell her everything instead of her searching through my stuff. Every time she saw me, she would claim that she didn't understand why I was there, I just looked too innocent.

Once she found out I was 17, it just amplified her reasoning, "You are just too sweet-looking to be here!"

My retort was always, "You are too beautiful to be here; you should be in some other country modeling. You don't look like you should be here either."

She was moved downstairs before me.

Once we got moved to the second and first floors, we could leave our cells for our meals. Everyone was trying to figure out who was who and why they were there. My next roommate would be deemed a true roommate as she was the best one I would have. It was her first time, too, but she knew the ins and outs and taught me what she could before she went to the hole. She was pretty, too, but she liked dressing like a boy. We would try to make a game out of our 10 minute shower that we only got on Tuesdays, Thursdays, and Sundays. We were given 10 minutes from the time we left our cells to disrobe, shower, clothe, and be back inside our cells. Rita was a "helper," meaning she would assist the guards with little duties or pass items out to us. When she came and opened our cell door after it had been unlocked, I made the mistake of being shy my first time and didn't get to shower. After that mistake, I just followed the routine: strip when you're supposed to strip so you can get it over with. Kind of like being raped. The more you fight, the harder it is on you, when you can just lay there and it can be over with quicker. At least, that's always been my reasoning behind it.

Tenisha was my next roommate. When I asked her why she was there, she explained that she was a prostitute and didn't want to listen to her probation officer. So she got revoked because she didn't want her probation officer in her life. She had been to prison before and knew how to deal with it so she was fine. I asked her one day if being a prostitute bothered her, questioning her like a school child asking a teacher. She just explained to me that she just couldn't see herself having sex with someone without getting something out of it. She was going to teach her daughter the same thing. This could be a good thing or a bad thing. My dad tried giving me the same lesson but his approach was a little different. He would always say that marriage was a legalization of prostitution.

"Ché, tell me what happens when a husband gets his wife a gift?"

"I don't know"

"They have sex, that's what. So even though he is still married, he is still paying for pussy."

We were allowed to leave our cells for an hour to go outside. Our outside area was surrounded by brick walls and had a little patch for us to exercise. We got to go to the library once a week. Once the case managers figured out which facility was the best for an inmate and there was a bed available, they shipped that inmate out.

Of course, while I was at Ham during the summer, with no air conditioner or fan, there was such an overpopulation of women coming in that they didn't have room for all of us. So a lot of us stayed at Ham a little over our intended month. When we were ready to be transported to the next facility, we had to pack what few items we had. We were lined up and shackled, then led to a van that took us to Taycheedah. It was on the very edge of a city that was almost surrounded by a lake. The scenery was pretty and I was thankful to be driving through it. I knew that once we reached Taycheedah, there would be no more windows to see the sunlight, moon, or the way the sun glimmered off of the lake.

I couldn't quite gather my thoughts when we pulled up to Taycheedah with its barbed wire fences around the whole complex. It was like its own private city inside of a city. There was a red house in the middle of the property. To the upper right was an even bigger house that was dull and gray. It was almost the size of a hotel. There were walkways in between each of the buildings.

I just stared, trying to take it all in. There was a building to the far right that just looked so dark and menacing, "the max building." Below it was the kitchen hall, but to the upper right of the red house (Harriet Building) was this flat plain-looking building with two doors. It looked like one of those buildings that factory workers would come out and finally see the light of day (the dorms). We attended an orientation in the visitors' room that explained all of the buildings the Allen, Harriet, Dorms, and Max. The building in the lower left corner was pretty much what I would call the control center, where all the cameras were, the visitors' room, and the property room. Above the control building was a gym and school.

After orientation, we walked to our separate buildings. The majority of us went to the Dorms, and my poor roommate went to the Max building because she had more than five years. I walked into this building that, if you looked at it with no roof, was a complete square split in quarters, lined with metal bunk beds. In the center was the "bubble," a circular station that was attached to the bathroom/shower room. Each side was split up and color coordinated. There was an outside area that gated us into the dorms with two metal patio sets covered in rubber. The dorm building inmates ate with only the dorm building inmates. I tried to remember the things my dad had told me about prison, to stick with people who were "lifers" because they would know the ropes.

Correctional Officer Finestone was my favorite officer; she was really petite and down to earth. She didn't treat us like we were nothing. She treated us like we were still humans. I had met a couple of people, Chelle and Balt. Of course, I would meet the people who the majority of the population knew and were scared of. When Chelle, who was in her early 20s, found out that I was 17, she wanted to "adopt me" to make sure that I wouldn't get bullied. The majority of the women created faux families to keep themselves safe and others safe. This is how it got out that I was 17. Not too long after that, she was making a bet with one of the COs that I was. When he pulled my file, he couldn't believe it, but there it was in black and white. There was only one other girl who was a minor and she was there for stabbing someone almost to death. No one could understand why I was there at that age.

That officer also noticed that there was a mistake and I was supposed to be in the Max Building. This was like a death sentence, like being at Dodge almost. Inmates could leave to eat but were locked down in two-person cells the rest of the time. Inmates couldn't even get hot water from the faucet to cook noodles because someone had thrown scalding water on another inmate. I feared the Max Building because that's where the lifers were who didn't care about themselves or anyone else. They were there for the rest of their lives.

Chapter Sixteen

I started school, which was pointless because I was still ready to test out, which I later did. I was so embarrassed to receive my GED in prison; it felt like a walk of shame for me. Everyone else was so proud. Some of the women were in their 50s just getting their GED. I was just ashamed of myself because I wouldn't be graduating with my class, so no senior pictures for me, just this little ceremony in the gym.

After I got my GED, I got accepted into the AODA program. They were going to try something new this time that I would be involved in. There were four floors in the Allen Building and the recreational area was in front of it, so they watched what everyone else was doing. I thought that going into the AODA program would help me with my appeal. I truly believed that I didn't have a problem, and I was just going to walk through the motions. The way they decided to run this program was by segregating us from the rest of the population. No one thought that this could be done since we were in such an overflow.

We moved to the Allen Building on the fourth floor. The program hadn't started yet, but they had gathered us all together in two-person cells on one floor. My roommate was Denise. She never told anyone why she was in there and none of us knew. All we did know is that she had been there for more than five years. She had the most beautiful kids I could ever remember seeing. Before we started our program, we were put on lockdown. No one knew for the first four days what was happening. We couldn't even leave to shower. On the fifth day, the news finally came out. A couple of inmates had attempted to escape. One was caught in the barbed wire and didn't even make it over the fence, and the other two did but they were both found because they lost so much blood from their cuts that they had passed out. After they were found, we stayed on lockdown for about two more weeks. They let us out once to shower. Once this fiasco was over, we all moved to the first floor.

There were two different AODA groups. I was in Ms. Kelly's class, though we got another facilitator in a couple of weeks. No one liked the new facilitator at first because we felt like we should have Ms. K. This was Ms. Kelly's first time working with women. I couldn't understand the hostility coming from some of the women towards these instructors.

Some of the women felt like if the instructor didn't have their own drug problem, then they wouldn't be of any help. We were only allowed to intermingle with the other group because we shared the same common areas. We weren't allowed down their hall, like they weren't allowed in our hall.

At first, the Allen Building still had other inmates on the other floors, but eventually they cleared everyone out of the building. We were instructed that there would be no games, and if the counselor felt like you weren't progressing or taking the program seriously, then you would be kicked out. Most of the women didn't want to get kicked out because the parole board was coming in a couple of months and it would look better on their file if they completed the AODA program. Everyone thought once you completed the intense four-month program, they would be released, because that's what they were used to seeing. People started getting kicked out of the group left and right. We started with at least 20 women in our group. Ms. Kelly explained that not one of us could be in a relationship while we were trying to complete her program.

Once we started the program, we were completely segregated from the rest of the population. We went to recreation in the gym with the other treatment group. We weren't allowed to go to the chow hall, which meant our meals were delivered to the building. Since it was wintertime, this meant all of our meals were cold.

Ms. Kelly was a great instructor in my eyes. First, she wasn't scared of us. Second, she just wanted to help us, but she could see the maliciousness that some of the girls had. We had meetings every day for eight hours, and then the weekend was ours. Our group's sessions started getting really intense. It seemed like everyone wanted to know your deepest darkest secrets, with some of the girls revealing horrific details from their lives. For several group sessions, I felt like the pressure was on me to tell my secrets. I couldn't be there without having to be on drugs, prostituted, or raped—I had to be abused at some point.

I called the only person in Fennimore that would still talk to me, Candi.

"Ché, you don't owe them anything. Those women are just evil and you don't have to tell me or anyone if you don't want to!"

Right after that guidance, I told my darkest secret. I could feel everyone's eyes boring through me in disbelief. Denise by this time had adopted me, too. This revelation would be the end of our mother-daughter relationship because one of the girls had pulled me aside after our meeting to explain that she had been through the same thing. Her case wasn't as severe as mine, but she didn't understand her feelings. I just explained it like Kelly did to me, except I was doing it in a joking way.

This secret of mine divided our group into black and white with me on the white side. It seemed like none of the black women would talk to me anymore. Denise almost got in a fight with Linda, another one of our group's members, because she was twisting what I said. Things were getting out of hand. I wanted to leave the program. I wanted to disappear. I hadn't told anyone this secret. Not my family, not anyone, but I told this group about malicious women who have been abused to the point where they feed off of someone else's pain.

The next morning during our session, we were all told that whatever was said during group was not to be talked about after the session, and if it you did, you would be asked to leave the program. Sheila pulled me aside after this session and told me that she knew that was the deepest darkest secret that I held to myself. She commended me for being able to tell someone because she knew what it felt like to keep a secret bottled up that no one knew. She explained to me that a particular person in our group just wanted to know everyone's business and she wouldn't give them the satisfaction. Then she told me how she got genital herpes at the age of nine because her father was prostituting her out and making her strip for his friends. All I could do was cry. I felt like I hadn't gone through anything at all. To be the tender age of nine when you are supposed to be still playing with Barbie and watching the Care Bears, my heart ached for her.

Eventually the 12 of us graduated from this program. Everyone kept guessing if we would get sent back into general population or stay at Taycheedah. Ms. K told us that she wanted all of us to go to minimum security because she didn't feel it would be helpful to throw the lambs back in with the wolves, so to speak.

Once we went back to general population, I was put on the south side of the dorms. The day I went back to the dorms, I ran into Mandy. I met Mandy when I was at the Grant County jail. We would pretty much spend our whole sentence with each other. Of course, the day I arrived, she found out that she was going to Burke, a minimum security center. There were two other minimum facilities, R.E.E.C. (Robert E. Ellsworth Correctional Facility) and John C. Burke Correctional Facility. One was for school, the other was for work. I wanted to go to R.E.E.C., and requested to go to R.E.E.C., but a week later, I was also sent to Burke.

Chapter Seventeen

I remember walking inside Burke for the first time. From the outside, it looked like a little business that was one story tall. There were two entrances. The first one was for inmates only. There was a stopping point where I was frisked when I came in from the outside. The second was for everyone else. There was a little entry way that led to the property room on the left and on the right was the case manager's office. There was a second door that opened to the cafeteria. It reminded me of a school cafeteria by its size and all the tables in a row. There was another door that led to an outside area that was enclosed for outside visits during the summer. Once I walked through the cafeteria, there was a crescent moon-shaped control room that was called "the bubble."

I stood there wide-eyed trying to grasp everything. The gated fence wasn't as high here and there was a huge field in the back of the building with a baseball field. We were allowed to have our own clothes here, not these stale body-odor uniforms. They lined us all up along the wall in the bubble. Facing it is where all the rooms were, and the officer told us which range we were in. Some of us were on the upper level and the rest were on the lower. The letters C, D, and E were above each of the halls.

As we walked down the hall, everyone started coming from their rooms because the count was over. As I went down the C-range hall to figure out what room I was in, a big burly woman brushed past me.

"What room ya in?"

"Umm…210, I think?"

"Ugh, ah Reed, I got a fucking roommate, can you believe this shit!?"

Nice to meet you too, I thought. The room was almost at the end of the hall on the right. The doors were wood, and finally there wasn't a lock that I could see. When I finally reached the door, I saw her name, and I thought it was a joke. It had to be a joke. The paper name plate said Ruby Flowers. How could the burliest of women have such a pretty name? I put the bedding that I carried in on the top bunk and tried to get situated. I went outside to take in the new area, where the majority of the women smoked their cigarettes. There were a lot of women around Ruby.

A couple of minutes past and I saw Reed coming towards me. I guess Ruby sent her so that I could learn my place. I just sat and nodded along to everything Reed told me about Ruby, as if I was paying attention. *Who the fuck did this bitch think she was! Did she run the whole center?* Yes, she did. I was fortunate enough to room with the person that the majority of the center, except the women who were completing life sentences (lifers), feared. She had also been there the longest besides the lifers. When I went to my room for count, she told me not to touch her things and we wouldn't have a problem. I thought that meant she wasn't supposed to touch mine either.

She started asking me what I wanted to do with myself. I told her that I wanted to go to R.E.E.C. so that I could go to school; for what I had no idea, I just knew that I needed to go to school. She told me that if I wanted to get a good job like working on the railroad, that I should work at the creamery. She also explained what places not to work at because there was no point in working at them. By the time you paid the institution your rent for the month, you wouldn't have any money left over for yourself. That's why it was important to get a job at the railroad, or at one of the larger factories. Everything else would be pointless. I filled out a slip to my case worker telling him that I wanted to work at the creamery.

It wasn't even a week before I started working at the creamery packing up milk for all the institutions and loading up all the trucks for deliveries. It was only for a couple of hours a day. Ruby told me for sure that I would get a real job by working there; that's how her girlfriend got her job on the railroad. I met Mister (astonishingly Ruby's cousin) working at the creamery. She was a real sweetheart and probably the only person who wasn't scared of Ruby. After a couple of weeks of working at the creamery I started a schedule of getting up early in the morning to work and coming back in the afternoon and taking a nap. Ruby had her way of waking me up for count by punching me. I didn't understand why she thought this was an okay way to wake me up. Eventually I would muster up enough courage to tell her that she couldn't keep putting her hands on me.

"I might not be able to beat you up, but I'm not going to let you keep punching me like I'm a punching bag. So please know the next time you put your hands on me we will both be going to the hole."

To my astonishment she stopped putting her hands on me. As she was walking out the door, she turned to me and explained that my panties shouldn't look like they did.

"I don't know if that is how those panties came because none of us get new panties when we come here, but if not, your panties shouldn't be looking like that and you need to the see the nurse."

That's exactly what I did. She was right: I had yeast infection.

I went to talk to Sheila and Jillian about the encounter I had with her. Sheila was appalled. I was still concerned with how to take the medication, but being self-taught was the Ché way of doing things. Sheila could have cared less about me having an infection that was common among most women. She was concerned with why my roommate was looking at my panties. They weren't out in the open for her to find. She had her side of the locker and I had mine. I would stay oblivious to all of the comments that Ruby would make to me.

"You should seriously think about being a lesbian. With men, they could have anything and give you anything, but with women there will be signs—discharge or an odor. Plus a woman can't give you an STD."

I would ignore all these comments.

Chapter Eighteen

When my grandma came to see me for the first time at Burke, I asked her to stop at the convenient store that sent clothes to the inmates. She sent me the clothes when she finally came up to see me. It seemed like Ruby was jealous of me having a support system outside of the center. She complained how she had to save up for everything that she had. I picked up the hobby of crocheting like a lot of the women did. If you weren't working a full-time job, there wasn't much else to do all day except playing cards, watching TV, reading, walking around outside, or going to school. Since I had already received my GED, if I took an employment class I would be able to receive my high school diploma. There wasn't much else to do at that time, so why not. I was still a little bitter that I wasn't able to go to Reel. After about six months of staying at Burke, I wanted to leave. I didn't feel there was anything else for me to accomplish here, especially after the showdown between me and Ruby over a pack of cigarettes.

She went to the hole and didn't think she was coming back, so she gave me her cigarettes. A month later when she did come back, she wanted her cigarettes. I tried to borrow them from someone, but we only got canteen once a week. The majority of the smokers didn't smoke the name-brand cigarettes. When I told her I couldn't get them, she went to Sgt. Button and told her that I stole them. I was coming back from the creamery when I was confronted by this woman screaming at me like I had just killed her dog.

"How could you do that? Why would you steal someone's cigarettes? I'm writing you up for this."

There was a due process besides her turning the whole center on me. Sgt. Button told the captains that she wanted me to go to the hole for this incident. I couldn't even believe that she would take it that far. I hadn't been in any trouble since I started my sentence. This would be the determining factors for Sgt. Button and captains who were respected.

You might not like a person or their personality, but if you were consistent and did your job, you were respected. We only had a few of them that were. The rest of the officers like Sgt. Button felt like they were working at a soap opera and were nosy about everyone and had no respect given to them and it showed. After a month, you could familiarize yourself with the voices that come from the bubble, especially when count was called. If you heard Sgt. Train, Field, Nohrs, or Stein, you knew no matter where you were you only had two minutes to return to your room for count. It took everyone else 10 minutes to get us all in for count.

Everyone at the center knew that Ruby had Sgt. Button wrapped around her finger. She got her to make me give the cigarettes back and moved me out of her room. It was a good thing that I only really hung around the girls who

I had completed treatment with and girls who worked at the creamery. Dee had this look on her face that was a permanent "I hate the world and everyone" expression. I never saw her smile, not once while she was there. She told Mister what happened between me and Ruby, and Mister wasn't having it. I got moved into Miss Candy's room. The first thing she said to me was not to touch her things.

I couldn't believe it, *now I was a known thief, after she gave me something?* We didn't really talk too much for the first couple of days, until all we could hear was screaming coming down our hall. Everyone was coming in from count. I could clearly hear Ruby's voice bellowing down the hall.

"You are going to choose that little bitch, over family! That bitch is a thief and she stole my shit."

Mister's room was right next door to mine.

"Ruby, I'm not scared of you like all these other females in here. You don't intimidate me. Stop lying on the girl. You know damn well she ain't stole shit from you, so stop lying."

"You can't tell me what she did! You acting like you want some!"

"I can tell you what she did, because I work with her. If she is such a thief, then why is she just now stealing something, huh! The shit don't even make sense, you just wanted her moved out your room, that's it that's all."

Miss Candy was at the door with it cracked. She turned to me as I was trying to read a book.

"Well, maybe I was wrong. Are you just going to sit back and not say anything when you know they are arguing about you?"

"I can't do anything they are both two different people. I didn't tell Mister to check her for me, that's why I didn't even want Mister to know."

"You need to do something, girl, before they fight."

I got down from my bunk, and poked my head out the door. Sgt. Button's voice came over the intercom.

"Tathers, you need to get ready for count."

If this wasn't fuel that started the fire.

"Sure, I will as soon as you tell Ruby the same thing! She should not be getting special treatment because she has you wrapped around her finger"

"You really willing to get fucked up over this girl, Mister?"

Ruby, you ain't gonna do shit! But bust your gums, you got everyone in here scared but I'm not scared of you, so step up then!"

"You come here then, I'm right here"

"Mister...Mister." I whispered in the middle of screaming and threats she turned to me with her normal sweet kind face.

"Yes, baby?"

"Please don't argue with her. I don't want you to go to the hole" I was so engrossed in the argument that I didn't hear Sgt. Button's keys as she came trotting down the hall. I looked up to see her grabbing the door and closing it in my face.

"Get in your room," she snarled at me.

I could hear her start to whisper to Mister trying to get her to calm down. I just lay on the bed. Count lasted an extra 10 minutes due to the argument because they hadn't started counting because everyone's door was open. When count was over, you could hear everyone rustling down the hall. Miss Candy had gone to the door and as she opened it to go out Ruby pushed the door open.

"I can't believe you turned my cousin on me; next time fight your own battles," she said as she disappeared into the crowd that was heading back outside.

Miss Candy turned to me, "She must have really liked you."

"What do you mean?"

"Well, you two obviously were diking." Diking in our definition at that time meant that a woman was in a relationship with another woman emotionally or sexually. She meant the latter.

"No, we weren't diking. She's with Kandyce and she's also not my type."

"Oh, I get it. You must not know that every woman that ends up being her roommate she messes around with."

"Except for me, huh."

"Well, now I see why she was so mad because she wanted some and you didn't give it up. You didn't really steal her stuff did you?"

"No, I didn't. I don't have a reason to steal anything."

Miss Candy started leaving her drawer unlocked because she knew I wasn't a thief. It wasn't even a week before Miss Candy got a night job and was able to move into a single room.

My next roommate would be crazy and all I could do was throw my headphones on and drown her out. Thankfully, I got the call that I had been waiting for in early August.

Chapter Nineteen

I was called to the front to speak with my case manager. I sat across from a man that looked like he was overworked and underpaid.

"Ché, what do you think about working on the railroad?"

"Well, I hear its good pay. I wouldn't mind working there"

"Okay, yeah…you're pretty young, so you should be able to handle the labor. I'm going to recommend that they interview you, okay? Then it's all you from there."

"Sounds good."

He finally looked up at me from his piles of papers on his desk.

"The interviews will be at the end of this week on Friday." I didn't tell anyone except Mister that I had an interview for the railroad. It was the best job that you could get at Burke, the highest-paying job. It also held everyone's attention to see who was going to get the job and who would last.

Four of us interviewed for this job, and all four of us got the job. The secret was out for everyone that got interviewed. How much secrecy could an individual have when your name was being called over the intercom. They held the interviews in the cafeteria near the main entrance. I remember walking up in my greens and white slip-on shoes. A woman who reminded me of a rounded face, red-haired Jane Lynch was sitting at a table.

"Hello, my name is Beth. I'm with South Railroad. We are based in Granite. It's a privately owned railroad company. We are looking into expanding with Burlington Railroad."

I sat there intently listening as if my life hung in the balance. This would be the difference of me leaving with or without money. When she started questioning me, I was as polite as I could be. I explained that I was a reliable worker and learned very quickly. She explained that the position would be mainly labor and there might be days we would work over eight hours. I thought to myself—*eight hours away from the Burke Center, eight hours of freedom that I'm getting paid for*—I could live with that. I had no idea what the real meaning of a laborer was, but I would soon find out.

I was so excited to tell my grandma that I got a job and she wouldn't have to send me any more money. The little money that I had been earning at the creamery paid for my basic needs. I usually didn't get ice cream, chips, or soup noodles like the rest of the women. My grandma had done a lot for me through this whole experience. I felt horrible that I was dragging her through this.

"Ché, I'm glad you got a job, but are you sure that's what you want to do? I mean it sounds like it's going to be very heavy labor."

"I'll be fine; they even pay 11 dollars an hour! The best part is I won't be stuck here all day!"

The minimum wage at that time was $5.15. I felt like this was the best deal I would get in my life.

"Well, Ché, if that's what you want to do, then do it."

"Now I won't have to ask you for money anymore."

We went shopping for work clothes the next day. There was nothing more embarrassing than going to a public store in your prison uniform and everyone knew where you were from because of your attire. I was so excited to get this job, after having what seemed like the roommates from hell. I was going to get my own room. The only time an inmate was graced with a room was if she was working, working a third-shift position, or had been there for over two years. Now that everyone knew who got the jobs, the bets started. Angel had just gotten to Burke. She wasn't even there a month before she got the job. She refused to work in the kitchen and wouldn't work any other job. Everyone was betting that she wouldn't make it a week. I didn't think she would either, but you never know, maybe she would. Sgt. Max later told me that they bet I wouldn't make it a week because I seemed too prissy. The one person I did know wouldn't make it was Shannon.

Some of the girls who had worked there the previous summer were still there after their release. We started orientation and then went out to the site where we were introduced to all the tools that we would be using. The first couple of days were just picking up railroad plates and spikes, but the second week was horrendous. We finally started on the rail and the first thing that we had to do was plug the ties. If they had previous spike holes, we had to plug them up with little wooden spikes. Sounded easy enough, right? The tool we used was called the plugger. It was a small pole with a thick circle metal block attached at the bottom and couldn't have been more than three pounds all together. But repetition made that three pounds turn into 30 pounds. At the end of the day it felt like 300.

Mitch was the new recruits' supervisor. He had been working for the railroad for almost five years. The other employees resented the fact that he was a supervisor at such a young age and for the amount of time that he had worked there. He showed new hires everything that we were supposed to know. Our first day was spent familiarizing ourselves with the tools we would be using. He also made sure that if one person was burnt out on a single project to switch us in and out.

It was only our second week, when Shannon quit. Mitch told her to switch with me because I had been plugging for the majority of the afternoon. She told him she couldn't do it anymore, which left me to finish until our shift was over and the van came to pick us up. I'm not sure if Mitch reported that he didn't believe she would be physically capable of performing her duties, or if she told her case worker that she wanted to quit. It was only Marilyn, Angel, Carol, and me at the end of the season.

The railroad job was a seasonal position and before the season ended, I had a hearing with the judge. The charge for first-degree conspiracy to reckless endangerment had been overturned in the appeal courts because it wasn't a valid charge. I took this opportunity to see if I could get an early release. I stayed at the main building where we met everyone before we set out for the day. The morning waiting it was dreary out, but I had hope that it would brighten up. Once the call was connected with the judge, I told him all the good things I had accomplished, volunteering for a couple of domestic violence issues while at the Burke Center, gotten a job—at the age of 19 I had learned my lesson and was completely rehabilitated.

"Well, Ché, that's why I sent you there so you could get yourself away from all the bad people in your life. I'm not going to give you a sentence reduction based on your good behavior or the fact that the charge for reckless injury was dismissed because you need to realize the seriousness of the nature of your crime."

I stood there in my steel-toed boots, feeling like they were cement boots. I couldn't believe that he was telling me that everything that I had done was for nothing.

"I also want to explain to you as well that the district attorney can charge you with a different charge that will be valid in the court system, so you might want to keep that in mind for your future sentence modifications request."

I couldn't believe what I was hearing. Did they hate my dad so much that I was going to have to pay for everything that they didn't catch him for? He sounded so merciless as if this was the best option for me. He could have sent me to Teen Challenge. The results would have been the same. I hung up the phone and started trucking up the hill past the garage. It seemed like everyone was waiting to hear the news and they could all tell by the sullen expression on my face. I just felt beaten down like nothing that I had ever worked for or done had mattered. The van came a little late that day, and I thought to myself, *if I really wanted to leave I could. I could just walk away from the garage. People would just think I was a construction worker. What would the good in that do?*

Eventually, I would get caught and, if not, I would always be looking over my shoulder and I didn't want to live like that. My dad had lived his whole life like that, and I knew that wasn't what I wanted out of life. I kept thinking my job wouldn't be so bad either, if I didn't have to keep paying for Angel's mistakes.

She had a smart mouth, and it seemed like every time she used it, I got the worst assignments that everyone else refused to do. When she mouthed off to John, I got assigned to move the plates under the rail. Being bent over for eight hours, I couldn't help but cry from the back pain. I didn't understand how they could even mix us up. I was smaller than her and wore glasses. She was a couple shades lighter than me and her face was round and mine was oval. The one thing that I did leave with from the seasonal job was that I had lost almost 50 pounds in a couple of months. I had never been so small in my life. I was always the little chunky fat girl in school. I came in a size 20, and after working those couple of months on the railroad in the sun, sweating and using my muscles all day, I was half my original size!

Most of the girls didn't bother to work during the off season. I took one temporary assignment. Colleen was the only one who decided to work during the off season. She helped me get the third-shift janitorial job. This meant that we didn't have to get up for morning count and we were on a whole different shift than the rest of population. I loved it; every night we would start cleaning the TV room first and then the bathrooms. Before the night was over, Sgt. Stein would take us outside so that we could smoke before we went to bed. I cherished these moments because Sgt. Stein talked to us like we were human beings. We weren't just another number to her, or someone that could just be abused and tossed away as some of the women who were getting pregnant by officers and captains.

I started seeing a psychologist during the last year of my sentence. After the incident with my drug counseling session, I knew I needed some type of help that my counselor couldn't give to me. I felt that I had all this free time on my hands with working the night shift and sleeping the majority of the days away. I remember Lilac like it was yesterday, with her round glasses and curly brown hair. She always wore floral dresses and brown sandals. She had an office in the nurses' station across the hall from the gym. Her office was only big enough for a standard desk, computer, and a second chair, but you could see the outside from her window. There were no bars, gates, or wires, just the outside parking lot and trees. Seeing something from the world that I used to know without that metal almost made me feel free inside. I continued to see Lilac just because I had nothing to do. After a few intense sessions, she had realized it was time for me to move on.

One afternoon, she was picking at her nails and I was getting annoyed because I thought she wasn't listening to me. She was. She stopped picking at her fingers and her hands fell to her lap. She suddenly crossed her legs, and looked at me.

"Ché, it seems like you're making some very sound good decisions in your life. Why do you keep coming to see me?"

"I don't know. I don't think the decisions I'm making are sound or good. At least that's what it seems like when I tell my family."

"Ché, I think that you don't have enough confidence in yourself and when you search for that approval from your family members, they still see you as a child. Not only do they see you as a child, they still want you to do what they want, not what you want. This is going to be the last session that we are going to have because I don't feel that there is anything else that I can help you with at this point dear. I know that it was unfair that you came to prison before you were even 18 years old, but you have to realize that you are an adult and are capable of making sound decisions. I don't see why you don't see that. Look, we both know that you don't belong here. What happened to you in that county was ridiculous and they should have not ever sent you here. If anything, I think this was more damaging to your development into an adult, but who am I? Ché, you have to make your own decisions from this point on and you can't always count on someone to be there to tell you whether it's a good or bad thing for you, especially if it's involving yourself. If there is one thing that I want you to leave here with today, it is you need to trust yourself. Okay?"

I sat there stunned, she had told me everything that I needed to hear and at the same time told me what I was scared of—that I could make my own decisions, I was an adult.

I felt rejected by Lilac, like I wasn't good enough for her anymore, but I soon came to realize that there were other women who really needed her help and I was just wasting her time at this point.

Chapter Twenty

Winter was here and this would be the last winter I would spend in prison. The holidays started slowly peeking around the corner. I hated the holidays, especially Christmas. Not because of missing my own family but it just seemed the season brought everyone's feelings down not being able to be with their own families. I was happy though because it was my last Christmas that I would be incarcerated. I was also happy that I was going to be able to do something nice for my family. No matter how much money you had, you were only allowed to spend $100 a month outside the canteen, but for Christmas this rule didn't apply.

You could spend $100 on your parent/child and $50 for grandparents/siblings. I had already sent my aunt blankets for her and her six children. I was still working on my grandma's blanket. It felt really nice to be able to get her something since she had been there for me through this whole process. I decided on getting robes for her and my step-granddad. I sent my mom and my brothers money, too.

My mom hadn't spoken to or written to me since I started my sentence. I wasn't sure if they had received their gifts, but one morning I walked into my room to see a purple enveloped card from my mom. This was the first letter or card that I had gotten from her the whole time that I had been incarcerated. She told me how grateful and surprised she was with the money and how she needed it at the time. She also told me not to confuse love with letters. *How ironic, that I sent you money for Christmas and now I hear from you. I'm not confused at all, that would mean that at some point that I actually believed you loved me.* I tossed the card on the desk. *How could she say that? Don't confuse love with letters.*

Well, if you cared about how I was doing, wouldn't you let me call you or write to me, giving me some type of support? I guess not. Winter was coming to an end and I couldn't wait for spring.

Spring was just around the corner, and I knew that I would be starting back at the railroad. I couldn't wait, because when we left the rail gang, we were at a lake. I didn't think they had completed it over that bridge so that they could move on, but I was excited to be back in the nature that those rails went through. Then Marilyn was called up front. The rest of us weren't called. I didn't know what was going on, whether I was going back or not, but during the break I worked at another company, so I wasn't really worried about going back or not. Angel was worried, neither of us got called to the office, so we weren't going back. She had to move from our tier immediately, but luckily I had the third shift position so I was able to stay in my room.

A week later I got called to the office. My case worker explained that they were having difficulties with some of the girls and didn't know if they were going to stay on as employees or not and that's why I didn't get called back. I started the week after Marilyn and Carol. I found it ridiculous that I was still paying for Angel's mistakes.

We didn't start at the lake like I had hoped. Instead, we were deep in the woods. We were all separated into several teams in between the machines. First, we had to take the old rail off. The first team followed this machine collecting the plates and plugging the ties back up or replacing the ties entirely. One side would be completed, then the next day the other; the rails were still being used, so we had to close them up every night. Going through the different towns and just being outside, I couldn't help think that this would be my life. Who would have thought I would be working on the railroad as a laborer? I started thinking about my release and had it all planned out.

I was only a couple of months away from being released. I would keep my job working on the railroad and go to school at night. I had no idea what I would be going to school for just that I would be going. I would get a little place of my own, and I would reveal my feelings for Mitch. We would eventually get married and have the cutest babies ever! A few things were wrong with this plan. When I mentioned to my supervisor that I wanted to stay on after I was released, she told me that she didn't think it was a good idea. Brew and Shimmy both went missing in action and Cassi was no better. All these women had been released in the past six months to a year. The only one that was still in good standing was Kate. She had just been released a couple of months before we came back. She was a year-round employee, not seasonal like the rest of us. My supervisor Anne said she wouldn't promise me a position, but that I would have to show her that I was ready to be committed to the company. I wasn't comfortable with an open-ended position that might end. I couldn't help but feel like my fairy tale ending had just popped like a bubble.

Telling my grandmother that I didn't want to move in with her like we had originally planned was one of the hardest things I have done. She had picked out what school she wanted me to go to and how I would get a work study position to make money. I just didn't think that was the best plan for me, following what someone else wanted me to with my life. I had listened to "I wouldn't steer you wrong" enough to end up here. I wanted to find my own way, with my own decisions. I knew that my grandma wouldn't lead me to prison, but I also knew that I would have done whatever she wanted and been stuck in a career that I hated, or not really finding out who I was. My grandma Adams on my dad's side told me that I wouldn't be able to please everyone and I couldn't live my life like that or I would be miserable. I let these words guide me with the hope that I would speak the right words to my grandma. *How do you tell someone that you love so deeply that you don't want their help anymore?* These were the thoughts going through my head right before count.

I had to call my grandma and finally tell her my plan.

"Hey, grandma, how are you doing?"

"I'm fine, counting down the days for you to get out. I'm so excited!"

"That's what I wanted to talk to you about, grandma." I hesitated for a minute. "I don't think it would be a good idea for me to come live with you. I appreciate everything that you've done for me while I have been here but I just think it is time for me to stand on my own two feet."

"Well, what do you plan on doing?"

"Well, I was thinking I could go to school out here and keep my job at the railroad. I'm hoping after this season that they will hire me full-time."

I was thinking her silence was a good sign. I hadn't ever disagreed with my grandmother, so I didn't know the signs to look for. Silence was not a good sign.

"Ché, you have to be out of your mind right now. Do you know how much money I've spent on you? You waited until right before you get out to give me this news, after me and my husband have rearranged our lives for you? What happens if you get fired from that job? What if they don't hire you full-time? What are you going to do then?"

I had completely turned away from the bubble and started pushing my face into the cement wall. I was so embarrassed to cry in front of everyone. I had not ever heard so much pain and anger in my grandmother's voice. I didn't know what else to say. I wanted to fold and tell her that it was joke that I was just playing around and couldn't wait to see her when I got released, but instead I stood my ground.

"I guess I will figure it out if that happens, I just want to be independent and know who I am

"Fine, Ché, fine...go be independent, see if I care. Don't call me anymore! I don't want to hear anything else from you!"

I had heard the officers call count a minute before, but I scanned the area around the bubble to see how long I really had. People were still on the phones downstairs and cooking food at the microwave. The tears were bursting through my face. I could feel it turning red.

"Grandma, please...." the line went dead. I turned to the bubble and there was Sgt. Cyanide mouthing for me to get ready for count. I couldn't believe her audacity. There were still people cooking their food, but you turn the phone off! I screamed my thoughts out to her, I couldn't believe it. I just stormed down the hall to my room. Everyone's door on Echo was open, waiting to see what was going to happen. The girl across from my room came to her door.

"Ché, are you crazy! Why did you do that! I can't believe you did that! What if they send you to the hole?"

"I know they are going to send me to the hole; it was Sgt. Cyanide I screamed at." I just sat there waiting for the inevitable.

After 10 minutes, they still hadn't cleared count. I knew then I was going to the hole. I guess I didn't have to worry about whether I was going to have a job or not because it was gone now.

Sgt. Cyanide came to my door, "You know I'm going to write you up for what you did, that was inappropriate."

"I don't care."' I just started screaming at the top of my lungs. None of it mattered anymore. The job, getting out, nothing mattered to me except my grandmother shutting me out of her life like I was nothing. The one person that I loved and supposedly loved me unconditionally had just told me they didn't want to hear from me ever again.

Capt. Kitty came to my door, "Ché, you need to come with me, you can't just act out like that. I won't have it at this center disrespecting a sergeant like you did. I thought to myself, *I could take this bitch but where would that lead me?* I decided to just say nothing. As we went to the first floor down to the red room, the reality of me going to the hole came then. They had finally cleared count, which meant shift change was done.

Sgt. Stein came to the door, "Ché, what size uniform do you wear?"

I could only hang my head and tell her XL.

She came back and had me strip. "You know the drill: lift your breasts, squat, and cough twice."

Once I was dressed, she came back and shackled my ankles and hands. I felt numb like I had felt the past couple of years of my life. Walking to the van all, I could think about were the last couple of words my grandmother spoke to me. I had to be transferred back to Taycheedah, none of the minimum security centers had a hole. The hole wasn't what I had expected it to be. I was in my own cell that had its own shower and toilet. You were only allowed outside for 20 minutes every other day. I was suffering from the conversation that me and my grandmother had. I spent my time thinking about what I was going to do now that I had just lost my job. I had been sentenced to 11 days in the hole.

The one thing I did like about going to the hole was there were a couple of officers that I wanted to see before my release date and I saw them both although they weren't too excited to see me. I would always be the 17-year-old that came to them. It was almost like motherly instincts took over. I chatted with them both, Finestone and Michals. We talked about what I should do and how they didn't want to see me again. I don't think they realized how they touched my life by treating me like I was still human, still a person with thoughts and feelings. It's very rare to find this type of treatment especially at Taycheedah.

After the 11 days were done, I was shipped back to Burke. I had less than three months before I was released. I didn't care if they made me stay the rest of my time there. There was nothing really left at the Burke center for me now. Everyone that I went through treatment with had already been released. I thought about what I was going to do, now that I had lost everything again. Where would I end up now? The only option left was to call Dad.

The first thing I did was smoke a cigarette. When everything gets taken away from you the little things make you happy, like smoking. Everyone was so happy to see me back, but couldn't wait to tell me how stupid I was because I had just lost the best job that was offered. I wasn't sad that I lost the job. I was happy that I got to see Finestone and Michals. I told everyone how Michals was pregnant.

"What are you going to do now."

"I'm just going to go day by day." I realized that working on the railroad had taken over my life and maybe going to the hole wasn't the worst thing in the world. I had lost so much weight from working there that I was half my original size. I laid around for about a week. I had over $3,000 saved up from working. I wasn't stressing about money, plus I had waited to file my income taxes. Burke had another thing coming if they thought they were going to keep my income taxes in their own account. They required everyone working a real job to have their refunds deposited into their accounts instead of giving it to their families. I laid around for a little bit, but eventually got bored with doing nothing. I had already crocheted Afghans for everyone in my immediate family. The only one I kept was the one I made for myself and if I didn't finish it I wouldn't have to send it out.

Chapter Twenty-One

Candi came to see me, which was a surprise, a couple of weeks before I got out, and said she would pick me up on my release day. Since I had no idea where I was going, I had nowhere to send my last blanket. My poor little plans had been flushed down the drain because of my own actions. My father reminded me that the last three months were the worst. It seemed like all eyes were on you because you were about to get released. I couldn't believe it, but I had been a good case. I hadn't gotten in any trouble, except for the stealing incident with Ruby. I was able to get signed up with one of the outside crews that left during the day. No one knew exactly what they did, just that they left and went outside every day. I worked with a couple of girls walking through trails. I still couldn't tell you what we did. We were always driving around and walking through the fields just watching the world pass us by. We talked about what we would do when we were released.

I didn't tell anyone that I was getting out soon because people went crazy when they found out you were getting out. It was almost like once they knew that you were being released, they pushed all your buttons so that you would do something to stay. This seemed like the exact case with my last roommate. I had been put back into C-range. I couldn't escape this hall! My new roommate had just gotten there, and we got on each other's nerves. She hated that I listened to metal and rock. I hated that she talked to herself. I didn't want to get involved with anyone else's life or family. I had had my fill. It's hard to create a relationship that you wished you had with your own family with people who are emotionally damaged themselves. But maybe that's what made our bond to each other. In some shape or form, we all felt like the court system had screwed us. We had all been used or abused at some point, which made us all guarded and we could relate to each other on those notions. No matter what crime was committed, we were all here. I just didn't want to create another relationship that I might not be able to handle once I was out.

She asked me every question under the sun. I only answered one:

"Why do you listen to rock and roll?"

Her answer was, I thought I was white, ironically enough. I could only explain the way I knew best. I picked a song that I had written all the lyrics to and read them out loud. When I was finished, I explained out every line and how I interpreted it and how it fit into my life. She just couldn't understand why I didn't listen to rap. At that time, rap wasn't consoling for me. It wouldn't allow me to express how angry I was, or these feelings of losing control, and being railroaded. I can still remember sitting on the couch with Teri (dad's ex-girlfriend) and the video for freak on a leash from Korn came on. "Oh my god, they picked a great name. They look like freaks!" I found it funny because that's how I felt living in that town, like I was a freak of nature. How do you explain to a child that you are black? What seemed like a freak of nature to them. I thought I had gotten used to it but the reality is that I never did.

Once I gave Rosie this elaborate reason, she finally stopped nagging me about why I was there and when I was getting out. The day of my release was approaching fast. I had to come up with a solid plan still. I finally called my dad and told him I didn't have anywhere to go.

His voice crackled over the phone, "What's been up with you?"

"Nothing really. I just got out of the hole."

"What? What did you do to get in there?"

"I yelled at a guard"

"Man, Ché, I told you how this shit is. They will always try to pull you off your square especially once you've hit your last three months."

I sat there staring at the floor.

"Dad, I don't have anywhere to go."

"What do you mean? What the fuck do you mean you ain't got nowhere to go?"

I explained the last conversation I had with my grandma.

"Damn, Ché, you never fucking think do you? You better not start crying either. Call me back tomorrow and let me see what I can do."

"Okay." I had forgotten about Mary Anne, and it seemed like she was always saving us. From that time, he was left in the middle of the town with nowhere to go after he was released from prison, to staying in the apartments that she managed, to taking me in. The next conversation we had consisted of him telling me that Mary Anne said I could stay with her until I figured out what I was going to do with myself.

I hated the thought of returning to the very town that I despised. The night before you get released, which is only on Tuesday, you have to pack up everything that you are taking with you. I had packed everything up, except for the outfit that I was leaving in. I turned everything in the next morning, the navy-blue tee-shirt pajamas, their greens, and the beloved white Keds. Candi was there the next morning. I was still trying to curl my hair when they called my name. Angel popped out of nowhere, "Can I have your curling irons?" I couldn't believe her; this was another reason why you don't tell people you are leaving because they feel they are entitled to your items because you're being released and can replace them. I just gave them to her. I didn't have time to sit and debate with her about why I shouldn't give them to her.

As I stood in the entry way to the Burke Center with Candi, my case manager handed me cashier checks for the money I had saved up. He thought it was odd that my probation officer didn't request the money to be sent to him. I went straight to the bank and cashed them. It was a three-hour drive back to town. Candi was as curious as to what I was going to do with myself as much as I was.

First things first, I had to report to Todd my probation officer. I asked Candi to sit outside so I could go into my meeting alone. I sat in the waiting room waiting for Todd to come get me. The last time I saw him, he was telling me how he felt that I should have served seven years in prison. I heard a loud buzz, the door to the inside offices had opened and there stood Todd taking up the entire door frame. His brown dress pants hugged around his tummy.

"Come on back, Ché."

I got up from my blue-gray felted chair. It seemed like a mile to his office, even though it was just five steps. I followed him to the last door on the right. It was a huge office, bigger than the lobby.

"Well, Ché, have a seat. Looks like you were released with quite a bit of money. What do you plan to do with it?"

Go buy a pound of weed and set up shop in this lame as town I thought to myself, is he serious?

"I'm not sure, yet."

"Well, first thing I'm restricting you from is seeing your father. You two are now on a no contact with each other. You need to get a job within a month or I'm going to make you complete the rest of your probation sentence in prison.

How nice. I'm not even out for half a day and all these expectations.

How am I going to get all this accomplished with no car? It was not like there was a bus system or a taxi company that you could call. There was no type of public transportation in between the smaller cities that could range anywhere from a 10–60-mile drive.

"So do you know what you are going to do yet? Well until then, these are the things that I want you to do. I'm not going to have you do drug testing because I don't think you even have a problem, and it would be a waste of money on our part. Well, if that's it, then you are free to go."

"Can I still have contact with Cederic?"

"I don't see why not. It's not like you two can do much harm at this point. He still has five more years in prison, doesn't he?"

I thought to myself, *you should know, you were his probation officer then.*

"I will do a home visit in two weeks with you around five o'clock."

Oh joy. There were so many things I wanted to say but just sat there. He followed me down the hall and then took me to another probation officers desk.

"I need you to contact B and let him know that he has a no contact with his daughter."

"Yeah, I'll call him right now."

I heard the loud buzz again as the door opened. I just walked back outside to Candi's car.

"Well where are we going now?"

"I'm going to Mary Anne's house. It's a couple of miles outside of town."

"So have you thought about what you are going to do now?"

"Well, my dad said Mary Anne wasn't doing so well, so I figured I could help her around the farm until I figured things out. I just need to get a car."

I tried keeping in contact with Candi, but finally realized that she was only keeping in contact while I was in prison because she pitied me.

Chapter Twenty-Two

Mary Anne greeted me with open arms. She had another roommate who was an alcoholic and his room was across from mine, but he didn't bother me. I wondered why he couldn't help her with her farm and her house appraisals, but that wasn't my business. It also didn't take me too long to realize that he stayed drunk all day every day. Me and Mary Anne went over some ground rules of the house, which were pretty modest I thought , down payment for the phone bill, and no rent just helping out around the farm. I saw my dad the next morning for a couple of minutes.

His new girlfriend was pregnant and showing and I could tell he wasn't happy. He had just broken his leg and was on crutches. I thought about running up and pushing him in the gravel and throwing the crutches into the pen with the Emus, but before another thought could cross my mind his voice bellowed.

"Stop acting all scary and come give your dad a hug."

My body went on auto pilot, and I couldn't help but think about everything that had happened between us up to this point. I tried not to blame him for my faults, but I couldn't help but blame him at times.

"I just wanted to make sure that you didn't get sent to a half-way house or no shit like that. I didn't mean to be so mad at you over the phone but now you're out!"

"You know they put a no contact on us, don't you?"

"Yeah, Cacey called me when you were still there to tell me that. She said she didn't have a problem with us keeping in contact but that she couldn't override what Todd's restrictions for you were."

He left after that, and I just felt so numb like I didn't know how I was supposed to feel. Was I supposed to be mad and fist flying as soon as I saw him? The one thing that did bother me was that I didn't bat an eye when a command came from him.

My first couple of weeks out I concentrated on keeping this new-found shape I had. It wasn't every day that a person loses half their size! I would run in the morning, help Mary Anne in the afternoons with her appraisals, and then be in for the night. My nights consisted of me writing letters to everyone that I left at Burke as well as Cederic and listening to music. I still had no idea what I was going to do.

One day when I was helping Mary Anne with an appraisal, I ran into Erin, one of my dad's old friends. I told him how I needed to get a car and he took me to his friends shop right outside of town. I obviously didn't realize what a salvaged car meant at the time, but I was so happy to be driving a two-door Saturn it didn't matter. I knew this was the car for me. I bought it right there and drove back to his house. I still didn't have my driving license, but that didn't stop me from driving home.

This was the biggest mistake, I could have made, not only financially but just being stupid. It was a forty-five minute drive back to Mary Anne's house. I had made it through Fennimore, which was a 40-minute drive. I thought it would be a great idea to take the back roads to her house just to make sure I didn't run into the police. Only a couple of more miles, I thought to myself and I would be home free, but then the radio starting cutting out. I couldn't stand listening to the static. It wasn't the original dashboard and I was trying to figure out how to tune in the radio. When I looked up, I was on the left side of the road and almost going off the road. I panicked and whipped the wheel to the right only to push myself into the right side of the ditch. I then whipped the wheel back to the left. The next thing I knew the car was in the air and my last thought was, *Oh, my God, am I going to die?*

The bright day had turned black. All I could hear was the glass breaking and the crunches from the car hitting the ground. When I woke up, I was upside down in my new car. I didn't understand what happened. I unbuckled myself and fell to the roof. The driver's side window was completely busted, so I climbed out. All I could think about was hiding the car and how I shouldn't have been driving it. I was holding my sandals in my hand as I pulled myself out of the wreckage. I couldn't believe I just did that. I was grasping the grass to climb up the side of the road. I turned and looked at my car. It didn't take a scientist to realize it was totaled. I totaled my first car in less than an hour. I started walking down the road. I probably made it a mile before someone stopped me and asked if I was okay. I didn't even realize that I was bleeding. The gentleman was nice enough to let me use his cell phone. I called Mary Anne and told her that I didn't know what happened, but I crashed my car. She told me that I had to go back to the car because they would consider it leaving a crime scene. All I could think about was the musty body-odor smell from the prison uniforms that I had just left.

"Ché, I'm going to come get you and we will figure this out when we see the car." Mary Anne found me a mile later.

'Ché! What happened to you!?"

"I was trying to turn the radio station and then I was on the side of the road and I turned the wheel and then the next thing I knew, I was in the air and then everything went black. I don't know I just I didn't even think…." My voice trailed off as we pulled up to where the car had rolled over. There was an ambulance and a police officer. Betty walked up with me to the officer.

"Is this your car?"

"Yeah, I just bought it about an hour ago."

"Do you remember me, Ché?"

I looked up and tried to gather some memory of where I would have known him.

"No, I'm sorry I don't remember you."

"Well, I was the officer who stopped you when you were walking down the freeway, after your boyfriend, what was his name?"

"Cederic?"

"Yeah, Cederic had just kicked you out of the car, and we pulled up. Don't you remember I used to be in the bowling alley when your dad's team would bowl? Man, your dad had a temper. I was there that night you came in and he just yelled at you all night, and then he slapped you right across the face." His voice had fallen with a hint of sadness.

"Yeah, I remember that night. I honestly just can't place your face."

"It's okay, well, can I get your driver's license?"

"Umm…I don't have one."

"Oh, Ché, you know what? I'm not even going to cite you. You've been through enough. You'll have a lot more to worry about when you report our contact to your PO, but you should really get to a hospital. We have an ambulance right here."

"No, that's okay, I'll be okay I don't have money to pay for an ambulance."

"Okay, well even if you don't go by the ambulance, you need to go to the hospital."

"What's going to happen with the car?"

"Well, we are going to tow it and then you can decide what you are going to do with it after that okay? You just need to go to the hospital right now."

Mary Anne explained that she couldn't take me to the hospital because she had an appointment, but she could take me into town.

"Don't worry about your face either. I'm going to give you some emu oil so that it doesn't scar bad."

As we got into town I had her stop at Brian's house. He wasn't home, but his brother was. As he walked up to me, I could tell he had been drinking.

"Damn, what happened to you?"

"I just rolled my car over. Is Brian here?"

"No, he isn't. I would take you but I've been drinking."

"What about Tiny?"

"He's been drinking, too. I'm so sorry."

I asked Mary Anne to take me to Stacey's house, my old best friend who was now engaged to my ex who came to the door speechless.

"Is Stacey home?"

"Yeah, hold on."

As he sat back down on the couch, he sarcastically asked what I had been up to.

"Oh, you know rolling my car in a ditch and totaling it. What about you?"

"Oh, I've just been watching TV today."

When Stacey came from the back of the apartment, her gasp told me that my face wasn't getting any better from waiting around.

"Do you think you could take me to the hospital?"

"Uh, yeah. Honey, can you watch Chelsea."

"Sure no problem. She looks like she really needs to go, and I don't have to go to work for another couple of hours."

"I'm sorry to bother you like this Stacey."

"It's okay. Are you ready now?"

"Yeah."

For the next 10 minutes, we talked about how much we had changed over the past couple of years.

Once we were there, the nurse came in to wipe my face. She placed a couple of strips of tape over my face to pull the skin back in place. I'm not sure if it was the near-death experience, but I called my grandma while I was there.

"Grandma?"

"What, Ché?"

"I just got in a car accident."

"What do you mean?"

I just totaled my car." My words were slurred while I was holding back the tears.

"Well, that's what you get. You don't even have your license. What were you thinking, and you just bought a car! You are going to go back to jail now watch. They are going to send you right back to prison."

My tears had dried up real quick when I realized that I wasn't going to get any sympathy from her. I was so hurt. I started screaming in the phone, "Well, thanks for caring that I almost died!" I hung the phone up. *Doesn't she know I almost died, how could she say that I would go back to jail?.* I didn't know what it meant to be on my grandmother's bad side, but I was about to find out.

When we got back into town, I couldn't help but stop at my dad's. When he opened the door he already knew what had happened.

"How'd it happen? You were fucking around trying to get your cigarettes weren't you? Why couldn't you have waited? Now look at your face, Ché, it's fucked up and now you are going to have scars on your face."

I just stood there hoping to be consoled, but this was being consoled from him.

"I'm just glad you are alive."

There, that's what I had been waiting for. *What was I going to do now?* Half my money was gone and I didn't have a car. I said my goodbyes to Stacey. I hadn't forgiven her for dating and later marrying my ex, but I knew deep down he wasn't the man for me. I wished I could tell her that before I got out of the car, but I just didn't know how as she dropped me off at Mary Anne's.

Mary Anne confronted me with all the messages that I had gotten from my family when I got through the door. I sat at the table and called my aunt back.

"Who do you think you are, Ché? You can't just hang up on your grandmother! How disrespectful!"

"You know what, Auntie? I almost died so I really don't care right now about how anyone feels about me hanging up on grandma. How could she be so merciless and say that I was going to go back to prison!"

"I think you need to talk to your mother, because something is wrong with you. How can you even have the audacity to speak to someone who changed their whole life around for you?"

"Changed it how?" My chest was heaving with anger. "I don't have time for this. I'm going to hang up now. Is that okay if I hang up now?" I didn't even wait for a response as the phone went back on its hook.

I called my mom a few minutes later. I hadn't spoken to her in years. Her voice sounded so docile and loving.

"Ché, what are you going to do?"

"I don't know, Mom. I really don't. They put a no contact with me and dad so I really don't have anybody here."

"Why don't you come out to Portland?"

"Is that where you are now?"

"Yes, it's really nice out here with the mountains. You'll love it out here. Just come out here and we can work on our relationship okay. What do you think about that?"

I thought that sounded like the most wondrous thing since my name was called over the intercom to be released.

"You can come out here and be with your brothers, get a job, and go to school."

"Okay, but I don't have a car and my money is almost gone now."

"Well, just get a job until you save up enough money."

"Okay, I love you, Mom."

"I love you too, Ché." I hung up feeling like even though I had just wasted almost $2,000 it was almost worth it since it brought me and my mom back together.

The next morning, I got a call from Todd.

"I heard about your little accident last night. You are going to have to come in to the office and drop. I just want to make sure that you weren't drunk at the time of the accident."

"I don't have a way to get out there, so how am I supposed to get out there?"

"I don't know, I guess you better start walking."

Walk 15 miles! He has to be joking? Luckily, I did find a ride later that afternoon.

"I wasn't sure if you were going to make it, Ché. Well, I have some good news for you. I've decided to lift the no contact order off of you and your dad. I saw you walking through town last week and you just seemed so lost and sad. I realized that your dad is probably the only person that you really have here."

"Thank you. I wanted to ask you if I could move."

"Move where?"

"I want to move to Portland, Oregon, to be with my mom."

"Well, I don't have a problem with it, but you still have to get a job in the meantime. The paperwork could take months to go through."

"Okay." I left the office that day with a little more hope for myself and where I was going in life.

I got a job at Hardee's working in the mornings. I was just grateful that Helen had given me a chance, but my other supervisor wasn't so nice and made sure that I knew that she didn't like me. Her harassment got to the point where the other managers had to step in because she was going out of her way to make me feel uncomfortable. I just kept telling myself that I only had a couple of more weeks and I would be out of there. After I earned a couple of paychecks from Hardee's, I bought another car, except this time I made sure that I had a licensed passenger since I still didn't have my license, which was required when you only have your driver's permit. Eventually I would pass my driver's test and I was just waiting for the state of Oregon to accept me. Finally, I was approved and two weeks later I had packed up my car with all my belongings and left. I'd hoped I would never step foot in that god-forsaken town ever again. I didn't want to abandon my brother, but he had our dad and also the Miller last name so he wouldn't be as out casted as I was, or so I thought.

Chapter Twenty-Three

It was a two-day drive from Wisconsin to Oregon. I drove straight through Minnesota and South Dakota. I started taking breaks once I hit Montana. I enjoyed watching the scenery change staring out the window at the sunset or how it rose. Some of the scenery was so beautiful that all I could do was pull over and stare. There was no description that would satisfy my taste, it just simply took your breath away. I finally hit Idaho and almost slid off the cliff, as it was my first time of winter driving. It reminded of me how I panicked and totaled my first car. I stopped and took in the snow-covered evergreens as I watched the cars pass by going down the sloped road.

I was almost there. I had hit Washington and Oregon and was only a couple of miles away. When I stopped for gas, a man started heading towards my car. I told him I didn't need any help that I could pump my own gas. Who knew it was illegal to pump your own gas in the state of Oregon! It was a little past 2 a.m. when I pulled into Portland on Interstate 205. I kept checking the directions to make sure that I wouldn't get lost and I was taking the right exits. I finally found the exit for Foster. I took 82nd street to Duke where my mom lived in a blue-colored town home. I was so excited and scared. I hadn't seen my brothers for years. I knocked on the door so timid that a mouse couldn't even hear. I knocked again and then I heard my mother's voice bellow out.

"Who is it!"

"It's me, mom!.."

"She's here! Wake up, she's here!"

All of the lights started popping on in the sequence of where she was in the townhome, first her room, then my smaller brothers' room, the stairs, and then the living room. She nearly ripped the door off the hinges. She snatched me up like I was still two and gave me the biggest bear hug. All I could do was cry. I finally felt welcomed. She started pulling on my red-hooded sweat shirt.

"What's this? Are you still dressing like a boy?"

My brothers came around the corner neither looked happy or maybe they were just sleepy? I stayed up with my mom for awhile and talked as the boys went back to sleep. She told me how my probation officer had already come by the house to do the inspection and explained everything to her.

When you or anyone that you know is on probation, you have no rights and if your family is there to help you, well they've lost their rights as well. He explained that he would be able to enter our home at any point in time that he felt like. The police were allowed to enter the premises as they pleased with no search warrant. There were no weapons of any kind allowed in the home, especially fire arms. No drinking or drugs. I didn't like the sound of Enriquez. He sounded like he was going to be riding my tail through town. I had an appointment with him a couple of days later.

My mom came with me since I had no idea how to get around the city yet. We waited for him to come in the lobby and get us. He took us down two long halls where his office was, if you wanted to call if that. There was a desk and two chairs. There was no room in his office at all. We were packed in like sardines.

"Well, Ms. Clark, I had a chance to go over your file and quite frankly I don't understand why you're here, especially with this length of probation. You didn't cause any serious problems when you were incarcerated, so I can't imagine that you will now that you are out. I have to explain to you that everyone who is on probation has to go through BetterPeople."

"What's BetterPeople?" I asked.

"It's a place that helps you find employment, but it teaches you cognitive skills that you are going to need in life as well. You are required to complete at least their third goal. I'm not going to have you give urine samples. It's obvious you don't have an addiction to alcohol or anything else."

This would be my first and last meeting with him. A few months later, I was reduced to low supervision. I had to fill out a report each month and send it in.

The first few weeks of living there was a struggle. I found myself feeling the same as I did when I was a child.

Taking care of my brothers and being my mom's personal maid. I didn't even live with my mom for more than two months before she kicked me out.

Luckily, I found a mentor through the program she was in. Melissa was the sweetest thing ever. I loved meeting with her and getting all my feelings out. It seemed like she was my only friend. I had already started school and was half through the BetterPeople program before I started dating someone who was in the program. We both graduated together but being naïve seems to be a horrible trait. I didn't really understand that he had mental issues that he needed to be on medication for. I would brush off his statements, "I don't know what I'm doing here, don't these people know that I'm a prince! How dare they treat me in such a manner." He truly believed he was a prince from another country even though both of his parents were born here in the United States. I didn't have the courage to leave him until I moved into a transitional housing program for homeless youth. I had gotten into the program before the cut off age of 21.

I received a lot of help from the staff and other kids. We would meet once a week and go over the house rules and what we would like to do. I would spend many late nights conversing with Sunsong. She was so beautiful and reminded me of my mother because of her light skin. She helped me understand that I might be a felon but that shouldn't dictate the rest of my life. I started working two jobs, one as an officer manager and another as a street advocate, meeting a lot of people on the streets. What seemed to amaze me the most was that most of them didn't want to leave the streets. My relationship with my mom was getting a little better. We just had boundaries that shouldn't be crossed like living with each other. Her favorite line to tell people is that I went crazy when I was 11 and got my period. This is how I'm introduced to her friends and complete strangers. I thought all was well. I had gotten a brand-new car, had a small income, and school was going just fine until my first year in the Medical Technician program.

When I was released from prison, I started having unbearable menstruations. I didn't have medical insurance so once a month I had to bear it. But during that first quarter in my program, I hadn't stopped bleeding for at least two months and it was taking its toll on me. My hours got reduced at work. I couldn't study properly because I was worried about money. By this time, I had only talked to my grandmother once when she came to visit my mom in Seattle. I wasn't even in Portland a full year before my mom decided to leave again. So I was left alone with a few friends that I had made in the program.

I called my grandma and explained that I couldn't take care of myself anymore that I needed some help. I wanted to stay with her if that was okay. It seemed like the past had washed away like the sand on the beach with an incoming tide. I had to wait again for the paperwork to be filled out and for Minnesota to accept me as a parolee. I thought the timing was right. It only took two months for the paperwork to come through last time and my lease was up in that same amount of time. Right before I moved out of my apartment, I got a call from my 16-year-old brother.

He told me our mother had left him in Seattle and went to California. I was so poor I didn't even have enough gas to make the three-hour drive to go get him. I called everyone in the family and my aunt lent me the money to go get him. When Fiona and I got to the apartment, I hadn't seen anything like it. There was food on the stove that looked like it had been there for weeks. Everything was in shambles; clothes were everywhere. There wasn't a spot on the floor that you could even see the carpet. A part of me wanted to start cleaning. I couldn't let anyone see this apartment in this nasty state. Another part of me just wanted to get my brother and get out of there. My eyes kept sweeping over the living room, when a silky yellow afghan caught my eye.

"She left it?"

"She left what?" Fiona asked.

Tears were starting to build up as I moved closer to the couch. My brother had come from the back with everything he was going to take.

"Yeah, she pretty much just threw her and our brother in the car and left."

"Why didn't you go?"

"I told her, I was going to school. She said she would leave me if I went. When I came home she was in the car and handed me an envelope with my social security card and birth certificate and peeled out."

I had reached the couch. I started pulling up the massive king-sized afghan I had made for my mom. It took me at least four months to make it, and she just left it like it was trash, like she had been leaving me behind my whole life. I started taking a second look around the living room. She had left family pictures and frames of us. I grabbed a laundry basket and started loading some of the items in there. I kept asking myself, *How could she? What kind of mom does this? Just leaves their children?*

We packed my poor little coupe up as much as we could with memorable items. We had gotten back from Seattle (a three-hour drive) before she called me and told me to go get my brother. I had a flashback of when I was 11, and she had me call my grandmother to ask if I could stay with her and she told me no. My mom needed to be responsible for me and take care of me and always love me.

That summer, I was sent to live with my dad. It seemed like she didn't care who took me, just as long as I wasn't there. I asked my mom, how could she just abandon her son.

"You know, Ché, I don't have time for this. Can you go get him?"

It infuriated me that she had waited 10 hours before she told anyone that he was there by himself.

"No, I'm not going to get your son because I'm not his mother."

"Well, oh well, then call Auntie or someone and see if they will take him. I'm done with him."

If only I could reach through this phone and choke you. I flashed back to living on Third Avenue in Minneapolis. Right before my father came to get me, I was just sitting on my bed kicking my legs back and forth staring at the wall in the hall. My mom passed by my room.

"Mom, are you going to miss me?"

"No, who would miss a ravenous monster like you. That's why you grandmother didn't want you either!"

My tears fell onto my knees, I pulled them up to my chest, and held myself hoping that someday someone would want me. That was my last thought before I hung up on her. I could never forgive her for leaving my brother, never.

My brother moved in with my grandma. It would be another two months before my parole papers to leave the state (interstate compact) was approved for me to live with my grandmother. When I moved to Minnesota, I had high hopes to finish school and get a job. All of my mother's children were pulled together because of her actions. Her favorite son would also move to Minnesota to be with his father. We were all together again. I was going to need my family's support while being jobless.

On more than one occasion my grandmother had to remind me that I couldn't do what I wanted here. Just because they knew my probation officer on a personal level didn't mean that I could do what I wanted. I tried explaining the situation to her several times. I had been put on low supervision after a couple of months on probation in Minnesota. Their low supervision offenders has to meet every three months, the second Thursday of the month between the times 9 am to 10 am or 5 pm to 7 pm. If I missed one of my appointments, they would immediately call my grandmother. I couldn't just skip work or class every three months to make these wasteful meetings.

Once I reached the last two months of my supervision, I was almost revoked. If you are revoked or obtain too many violations, this basically means that you will be sent back to prison. Potentially, you could be sent back to prison for the whole duration of the time you spent while on probation/extended supervision. Being on low supervision wasn't the best option for me. I wasn't able to schedule a meeting when a time worked out for me and my officer. Not having an officer that knew me and knew that I was self-sufficient at this point in my life and that I didn't need to be micro-managed. When I requested to be moved back to having a single officer, my idea was rejected because I wasn't used to being on low supervision and was having issues adjusting. I couldn't believe their audacity. They would have preferred to revoke me then try to help me figure out a better time to meet with them. Then the excuse was that I wasn't used to low supervision even though I had been on low supervision the majority of my seven and half years on probation/parole.

When you were on low supervision, you didn't just have one person that you would see. There were several officers that you would see. They would all ask the same meaningless questions to me. Are you working? Are you still attending school? Do you have any questions? I couldn't always make the meetings because of my schedule. They didn't care that my school instructor locked the door after the start of class because you needed to be there on time or that I didn't have paid time off of work to come to the meetings. I had to be on drugs, because I wasn't attending my meetings regularly. Even though I kept requesting to have monthly meetings, I needed someone that would work with me and my difficult schedule. The low supervision officers didn't care if you had to miss work and got fired. They didn't care if you had class because they couldn't fathom someone like me having the ability to take care of themselves righteously. I though squatting and coughing was embarrassing, but having someone watch you urinate into a cup somehow seemed worse to me.

I began to understand why so many of the women that I was in prison with would rather finish their sentence in prison. They wouldn't have to be on probation when they were released, which gave me a new found respect for their decision to finish the entire sentence in prison. This meant they wouldn't have to jump through the hoops or have the fear of having someone else's hands. The horror stories like Sue finding a job and taking a vacation day without permission from her officer and then losing her job because she was in jail under investigation would stay with me my entire sentence. The majority of the women just wanted to get their lives back together and found it less difficult without a probation officer being in their lives discounting their efforts.

My family witnessed first-hand what is was like to have a felon in the family. How their rights are stripped away like mine. They lost their right to bear arms in their home. They would not ever be able to bear arms while I was in their home, even visiting because I am not allowed around fire arms for the rest of my life. The little enjoyments that no one ever thinks about, like having your husband's last name or the ability to leave the country. Not being able to go on a family vacation without prior approval from your officer. How hard it is for me to find employment and housing. I thought going back to school into the Medical Technician program that I was in, in Portland, would change my circumstances, but several things happened.

The first being the college I transferred to only took 6 credits out of 60. I had to start all over. Then after finishing a semester of pre-requisites to get into the program, I found out that they don't take anybody that has any kind of criminal background. I switched majors and finished with my associate's degree six years later due to transferring issues.

The most important thing I did for myself was see Cederic again. We had written each other the whole time I was out. I promised him I wouldn't leave him in prison to rot and I didn't. I was surprised to see him the day, I went to visit my brother. He had read on my Facebook page that I was going to be in town that weekend. No matter how you feel about a particular situation or how you left it, there are still some things that need to be said. I didn't even realize how I felt about him not testifying at my trial. And he abandoned me like everyone else in my life. He said he loved me, and cared about me, but he left me to get hung by that jury. He didn't want to testify because he was thinking of himself.

As the words were pouring out of my mouth, the tears were streaming down both of our faces. After I was done, he told me that he didn't know that I had felt that way. I explained to him that I didn't even know I felt that way as well until the words starting come out. I stayed by his side for his entire sentence, and all he did was tell me that his family didn't believe in my dreams, that I couldn't do anything, I wouldn't be able to work in the medical field, I wouldn't be able to get a good job. I knew that they blamed me for everything and they always would. He didn't understand what I now understood. He was infatuated with me. I had felt guilty for five years of my life because he wasn't able to enjoy life, but what I had to understand is that he also made his decision that night.

I didn't realize how much this conversation meant to me, how safe I felt in his arms even though I knew that he wouldn't protect me. He still couldn't understand my resentment for that town or that I knew he wouldn't ever leave it nor would he abandon his family. It was a conversation that I had been waiting eight years to have with him. He told me all the memories he had of me. Some of them I could only look and ask him if they really happened. I couldn't imagine being that person he was describing to me. He asked me a question that he had been waiting years for an answer. Before we both went to jail, I had passed out at work and when I went to the hospital they told me they ran a pregnancy test but it was negative. I just sat across from him in disbelief that I didn't answer his question, and thought to myself what would be the point of telling him the truth and decided against it. He had moved on with his life and so had I.

After having this conversation with him, I felt like I had the closure I needed from him. He was a big part of my life and now I could finally let him go. I didn't realize how angry I was with the whole situation until I had to talk about it. But now when I talk about it, I have different feelings. Maybe it's because I'm in a better place in life. Even though I have been told by lawyers and county officials that they will not expunge my record, I haven't given up hope. The court rejected my petition to expunge my misdemeanor cases because I was under the age of 18. I can no longer speak with my attorney that handled my case because he is now the district attorney of another county. It would seem that the state has covered its bases on shutting the door in my face. It doesn't help that in 2011 Wisconsin did not grant one expunge request. I haven't given up hope. I still dream that one day I can see Paris with my own eyes.

I believe in humanity. I believe in stopping on the freeway to make sure people are okay or to see if I can help. I try to pay things forward. I try to help people when I can in any way that can. If you asked the people that I've helped over the years if they knew I was felon, they would say no. They would describe me in a different manner than the district attorney in 2001, that I'm too nice and sweet to be a felon. When people ask me how I can still be so kind and sweet after going through what I've been through, all I can say is, "I'm just me." This entire time, I've just been me. I now hold a positive outlook on life and even though I'm rejected by apartments, employers, and people (after they find out about my past), I don't give up hope that one day someone will give me a chance. One decision can change your life, but it doesn't define who you are. That one day my grandma won't be the only one calling me, "The Best Little Girl in the World."

Made in the USA
Charleston, SC
04 April 2013